Response to *DNA of a R*~~~~ *lution*

F OR much of my pa~~~~ ~~~~ ~~like this.
Gary extracts the e~~~~ ~~~~ ~~ovement of Jesus
followers and captures t~~~~ ~~~~ ~~~ce of the early church in
Acts. The first church was ~~~~~ect, but by flexibly following the
Holy Spirit, these everyday disciples changed the world.

— **TIM ERICKSON**
Sr. Pastor, Bible Evangelical Free Church, Tomah, WI.

E XCELLENT, powerful, very well done. I need a box of these books
next week! This is not a book of theory, Gary writes from years of
encouraging and equipping leaders for the revolution. He allows us
to feel the rhythms and priorities that created a life-changing way of
doing life together on mission. He calls us from the program-focused
mind set to the integrated life of disciplemaking that exploded on
the first century world. DNA of a Revolution challenges me to not
play it safe.

— **STEVE HOPKINS,** *Group Leader: Bible Teaching and Leadership*
Resource Group, State Convention of Baptists in Ohio

D NA of a Revolution is for those who believe the Church is called
to be more than a critic of a deteriorating culture. It is for those
concerned that the Church is becoming an island of piety in the sea
of irrelevance. And, it is for those who still believe that the church
remains God's chosen vehicle to reach His world with the hope of
Jesus. This book you are holding will assistant anyone who recognizes
that the privileged place of "church" is passing yet the need for Jesus
remains. As a church leader I am picky about what I read, but this
is a book that fits our time and place at our church. Gary combines
biblical scholarship with practiced expertise and a heart that beats
for God's church to impact our world.

— **BOB THOMAS**
Lead Pastor, Calvary Church, Los Gatos, CA

I KNOW Gary thinks this book is for pastors and ministry leaders, but he's wrong. *Every Christian should read it!*

— **KEN MCMULLEN**
PROFESSOR, US HISTORY NUT, SANTA ANA, CA

G ARY has been helping churches recalibrate ministry for well over 20 years now. Here in this book he gives us a simple and straightforward way to connect with the energies that propelled the original church. DNA of a Revolution is a meaningful addition to the global conversation from the director of ChurchNext at CRM.

— **ALAN HIRSCH**
AUTHOR // ACTIVIST // DREAMER // WWW.ALANHIRSCH.ORG

THIS is provocative, challenging and encouraging. Gary doesn't just say we have a problem, but his whole train of thought is one of forward movement, contributing to the conversation in ways that are helpful and tangible. His chapter on mentoring the next generation of leaders is huge, especially for us young guys. What Gary has given us here is incredible.

— **TRAVIS COLLINS**
DIRECTOR OF MISSIONAL COMMUNITIES, NEWMINSTER: LONG BEACH, CA

F RESH, clear and easy to understand. This book is definitely not a regurgitation of something I have read before. I really like getting back to what Luke's tells us about the foundations and "DNA" of the Church. Let's look to the Bible to see what it tells us about the foundations of the Church—what a novel idea!

— **KYLE KALMA**
PRINCIPAL, CLEAR MEDIA GROUP: CORONA, CA

G ARY Mayes' remarkably engaging interpretation of Acts deftly combines expert "man on the street" straight-talk, with the wit and color of a front-line observer of the inner workings of the church. Few authors unlock the DNA mystery of the first century revolution in a way that compels the reader to join the crowds and take to the streets to bring the dream to life! Passion for the Church is splashed on every page and compels the reader to rediscover the genetic code that will splice each of us into the grandest revolution ever imagined.

— STEVE HOKE

CO-AUTHOR, THE GLOBAL MISSION HANDBOOK; LEADERSHIP TRAINER

I'VE served on several elder boards in local churches and I only wish I had a volume like this during those days. What Gary presents gives hope and an ancient way forward. It is of immeasurable value: easy to read, biblical, and practical—wisdom accumulated over many years of passionate commitment to the local church. If I had known—and lived out—even a fraction of what he describes in The DNA of a Revolution, I could have avoided a lot of pain. This book is of superb value for any local church serious about health, vitality, and being in the center of God's missional intent for the world.

— SAM METCALF

PRESIDENT, CHURCH RESOURCE MINISTRIES

GARY'S insightful reflections on the Book of Acts are immensely helpful in showing the church how to navigate the waters of cultural change. As someone who has worked with hundreds of churches and ministries, Mayes urges us to reclaim the values and priorities embraced by the earliest Jesus followers. He skillfully points the way forward by having us look afresh at the revolution that once was Christianity.

— MIKE ERRE, LOVER OF ALL THINGS OHIO STATE

SENIOR PASTOR, EVANGELICAL FREE CHURCH, FULLERTON CA

SELDOM have I read a book about the Church and ministry that has motivated me more to get past the warm fuzzy feelings of inspiration to thoughtful, eager action. As I turned each page of DNA of a Revolution it was as if I was given fresh eyes for The Book of Acts and an intensified desire to be the leader that God meant for me to be, to lend leadership for what the Church was meant to be – a revolutionary community that is legitimately the hope of the world.

— ED SALAS

PASTOR OF HUMAN DEVELOPMENT, NEWSONG, ORANGE COUNTY, CA

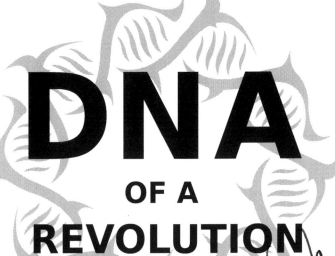

DNA

OF A

REVOLUTION

1st century breakthroughs that will
transform the impact of the church

GARY MAYES

LONG WAKE

Leaving a Lasting Imprint

www.longwake.com

DNA of a Revolution
© 2013 by Gary R. Mayes

ISBN-13: 978-0615878317
ISBN-10: 0615878318

First Printing: September 2013

Cover and Art Design by **Jason Loftis: http://jloft.com**

LONG WAKE
Leaving a Lasting Imprint
www.longwake.com

Lasting influence flows from the integration of who we are and what we do as followers of Jesus. Long Wake Publishing produces resources committed to both.

Contents

preface 11

Riding the Rapids 17

The Power of Mission 31

Getting the Who Right 47

An Apprenticing Community 65

More than an Organism 83

Explosive Multiplication 103

Diversity: Heaven in the Present 119

Decision Making and Authority 135

Contextualization and Courage 151

Generation Next 169

Spiritual Power 187

Reclaiming Our Birthright 205

appendix

About the Author and CRM 219

preface

As a freshman in college, God wrecked my life.

I went away to college to pursue my dream of becoming an architect and designing buildings that would inspire people with their marriage of beauty and function. However, before my second semester even began, the entire trajectory of my life was upended.

Not only did Jesus become unmistakably real to me, but as I listened to the stories of my fellow students, my heart broke over the lack of impact by the church among my generation. Whether my perspective was entirely accurate or not didn't matter. The Spirit of God used those experiences to ignite a passion and burden to shape the church that could be in order to reach the world as it really is.

I transferred to a Bible college, started serving in local churches, went to seminary (three of them), and began to live out this calling. Over the years I began working on broader levels with other pastors and their churches. These days I find myself in a leadership role over a movement that is transforming the impact of ministry leaders and their churches not only across the U.S., but in countries around the world.

The thing is, no matter where I lived and no matter what my ministry assignment looked like, that burden and passion born during my freshman year of college never waned. Forty years later, it is stronger than ever. I am more compelled to spend my life serving ministry leaders and their churches today than I have ever been.

We live in the midst of seismic change on every level of life. The very landscape beneath our feet is changing and these changes are fueling a global conversation about the way forward for the church. On every continent, ministry leaders explore questions about the nature, mission, effectiveness, and contextual relevance of the church in its current forms.

This book exists to contribute to that global conversation. While so much contemporary writing about the church addresses demographic shifts or explores successful church methods, this book is written to provoke fresh thinking about the church based on the events in the book of Acts. The journey of the early church brought them to critical turning points and junctions where they literally had to start over. Examining the formational impact of those moments reveals critical pieces of our DNA—the keys to the way forward for us in the twenty-first century. My experiences, biases, and perspectives certainly shape my contribution, but my goal is to spur conversation anchored in the Scriptures.

This book is written for every follower of Christ who believes the Church is God's primary delivery system of hope in a broken world and longs to see the revolutionary impact of the Church unleashed—the Church globally and the church locally. My hope is that pastoral staff teams, church boards, ministry teams, and small groups of committed Christians would read and dream and find the courage to act in new ways as they discuss this together.

My prayer is that those who are unsettled or even disenfranchised by the current state of the church would find in these pages the beginning of a new way forward.

People for Whom *Thank You* Feels Inadequate

I understand that for the majority of my readers, a list of characters like the one that follows can feel like the Academy Award winner droning on with names that mean very little to you. Yet, nothing of substance is developed in isolation. Without the insights and encouragement and tangible support that came from each one of these people over the past few years, this book would never have been finished. For each of you who had a part in this long-term project, your contributions have been priceless to me.

I cannot express enough gratitude to Tim and Tammy Cahill, Alan and Martha Caughey, and Keith and Lori Webb. At strategic points in the writing process each of you provided a place for undistracted writing and study. God used your generosity to break logjams and advance this project by leaps and bounds.

Ed and Ginny Salas, you two provide constant encouragement and personal support that keeps me in the game. Ed, your leadership over that wonderful community we knew as Tapestry gave me a place to test the initial concepts and framework for what would eventually become this book. Ginny, your constant faithfulness covering the administrative details of our work together at CRM gives me freedom to focus on all I do.

Many of you have read and commented and strengthened the content of this final product. You were gracious, articulate, and truly helpful. My deepest thanks go to that community of readers who spoke into the final product: Steve Hoke, Ken McMullen, Kyle Kalma, Mark Thrash, Travis Collins, Steve Ogne, Daleen and Bryan Ward, and Connie Kennemer.

The task of moving from writing to putting an actual book in people's hands happened because of key partners on the production level. Tom and Penny Erickson, you two made it possible to bring in the outside resources that were essential. Jason Loftis, you have been my technical and artistic partner for some time—thank you for giving yourself and your skills to this project. Ryan Dunham, your playful partnership was key to the brainstorming and business end of this whole publication thing. Cat Caya, I had no idea what a gift you would be on the editorial front. It is frightening to think of what would have been lost without your help.

My friends and colleagues at CRM and within ChurchNext in particular, I cannot imagine a more competent and godly crew of men and women with whom to hang my shingle. You call me to a deeper place as a leader. You infuse my limited perspective with bigger and better thinking. Your insights on the church, on leadership, and on what it means to follow the Spirit continually shape me. You draw my heart to Jesus. You make my work a joy. I love your willingness to dream and to give yourselves not just to the church that is, but to the church that could be. Of the dozens of you whom I could list by name, I think you will understand if I limit my named thanks to my leadership partners: Sam Metcalf, Wayne Harris, Tim Warkentin, Steve Ogne, and Tom Wilkens. I would be handicapped without all that you contribute to my life and work. Thank you.

And, to my ministry partners, you empower everything I do through your prayer and financial partnership. Day after day, I step into the room with ministry leaders because you put me there—because you are there beside me. This book and all the experiences behind the scenes that made it possible are another product of your faithfulness.

And to my family, there are not enough words. This book is really *our* project. You have no idea what it means to me that you actually think I have something to say. Your kindness and encouragement carried me as I wrestled, wrote, re-wrote, whined, and fought to find time over the past few years to bring this project into reality. I know that there were times none of us thought we would see this day, so thank you for your patience. Margaret, more than anyone else, your honesty, perspective, and partnership on every level make this book as much yours as it is mine. Thank you.

Gary Mayes
July 2013

one

Riding the Rapids

WET, sunburned, and loving every minute of a perfect July day, three friends and I were rafting the Snake River near Jackson Hole, Wyoming. Now granted, we could have opted for the upper section of the river—that portion where guides take the leisurely-inclined on barge-sized rafts for "float trips" through pristine waters at the base of the Grand Tetons. Not us. We wanted to live the postcard. We hired a local outfitter to take us down the wild section of the river that carves the rugged canyon south of town. We were college students looking for grand adventure. This would be a high point in our summer while working in Yellowstone National Park.

Three hours on the water taught us to work the river and work as a team. We were ready for anything as we came to the final rapids of the day. Man against nature, we braced for the fight. We attacked over the crests and splashed through troughs of turbulence. We were brash and bold, and felt like conquerors…until, suddenly, I was in trouble.

Ever been whitewater rafting? When it's good, you experience the raucous adventure of hand-to-hand combat against the raw power of nature. You paddle your raft around boulders, over waves, and into treacherous eddies that can swamp you without warning. It's exhilarating. It's intense. It's dangerous. These days, all rafters wear safety helmets out of respect for the dangers of the river. In 1976, no one wore helmets. That was the summer I discovered the exhilaration and danger of whitewater rafting.

I am not sure how it happened. Paddling hard over a ridge of water, I lost my balance. I may have leaned out a bit too far, been bounced by swirling currents, grown a little overconfident, or maybe all of the above. Whatever the cause, the result was the same. One minute I was paddling hard and in control, the next I was launching headfirst into the whitewater. I will never forget that helpless sensation of leaning past the point of no return.

Seeing my nosedive from his perch on the back wall of our small raft, our guide reacted instinctively. He tossed his paddle aside, commanded the others to hold him tightly, and stretched out as far as possible beyond the back of the raft in hopes that the churning waters would push me within reach. A flash of orange. His arms plunged deep into the water. His fingers found the edge of my life jacket and grabbed on tight. Our guide hauled me up into the raft and, without a blink of hesitation, he and my three friends resumed paddling, pulling hard to get us beyond the vulnerability of that mid-rapids vortex.

The only reason I know anything at all about the drama of my rescue is that my friends explained it to me later. I have no memory of being in the water. I only remember the initial shock of recognition that I was going overboard. My head hit something immediately and knocked me unconscious. Puncture wounds on my scalp and feet testify to washing machine-like turbulence among submerged rocks below. However, because I was unconscious, I came through it all without any trauma. My next conscious moment was when I awoke seated on the floor of our raft holding a bandana to stop the bleeding from a gash above my left eye.

A few hours, a few stitches, a few medical instructions, and some much-needed Tylenol™ transformed the whole ordeal into a legendary adventure—scars and all. Call me naïve or call me dense, but the danger of that "swim" didn't dawn on me until a long time later. The truth is, if those currents had pushed our raft a bit more to the right or the left, I would have been out of reach ... If one of the collisions between my head and those boulders had been a bit harder... If the churning undertow beneath those rapids kept me tumbling below the surface just a little bit longer... Well, you get the idea.

I tell the story of my adventure on the Snake River because I believe it parallels our experience in the church today. We are paddling our way through the rapids of disruptive change in culture, world view, technology, communication, economics, and so much more. We are trying to dodge rocks and currents of an unknown and unpredictable river we have never navigated before. Even though rafting an untamed river can be an adrenaline-packed journey of nonstop adventure, I am afraid that for a vast number of our churches, the journey we are on is life-threatening. Pastors and ministry leaders of all types, churches young and old, even whole denominations are being bounced out of the raft and into the rocks.

The rocks and eddies in our waters are no polite metaphors. They are real hazards causing real trauma to real people every day. Pastors are leaving ministry in droves and churches are closing their doors. There are no simple answers. We are traveling in uncharted waters where paddling back upstream is a luxury that does not exist. The days of doing business as usual are no more.

On that summer day on the Snake River, my friends and I needed a guide who would teach us how to navigate the twists and turns of a turbulent river. We needed one who would help us stay nimble amidst changing and unpredictable conditions. In the same way, the church today needs the strong hand of a guide. We need a guide who will do more than show us the way. We need a guide who will teach us to raft unknown waters and possibly reach out to pull us back into the boat.

We also need someone who will help us see beyond the danger, someone to remind us we are on a great adventure. Riding the rapids keeps things exciting. Being part of God's kingdom enterprise in a time of quantum change means amazing opportunities for ministry surround us. We are part of this miraculous organism called the Church—God's delivery system of hope for an uncertain world. To thrive in these waters, we need a guide who will help us keep perspective. We need a guide who will keep us from being swamped by our fears. We need someone to remind us that mere survival is not the goal.

This book is not that guide.

This book is an introduction to that guide.

Perhaps more accurately, this book is an attempt to reintroduce you to the God-given guide who has been in our raft all along. That guide is the first century church and the story of how she found her way through the uncharted waters of her early development.

What Would They Say To Us?

Allow yourself a little sanctified imagination. Picture a group discussion in the worn leather couches of your local coffee house—your favorite java-chino-soy-no-foam-one-pump-latte in hand. You and a few close friends are engaged in an unhurried conversation with the leaders of that first century church. You tell them about the challenges of ministry in the present day and asked for their wisdom. What do you imagine they would say? How do you think they would respond?

Think about it. That little band of men and women began with 120 people in an upper room and became a movement that transformed the Roman world. They lived with no manual on how to be the church. They were a powerless group of persecuted outcasts. They had no models of successful churches to emulate, no seminars to attend, no books to read, and no New Testament to study. They were navigating without a map and every time they turned around, they faced another disruptive challenge. To borrow from Robert Quinn, "they were building the bridge as they walked across it."[1]

If those leaders of the first century church could speak to the church of the twenty-first century, what advice would they give us? What would they want us to know? What would they dwell on and what would they skip over?

Would they outline strategies and philosophies of ministry? Articulate step-by-step methodologies for multiplying churches? Boil down the complexities and mysteries of the kingdom into a diagram for success? Teach us how to preach and plan worship services? Provide curriculums to transform our small groups or Sunday School classes? Create a congregational policy manual? Would they focus on the kind of answers or formulas we typically look for in the books we read or seminars we attend?

I don't think so.

They would tell us their story. They would tell us about the tenuous experience of figuring things out as they went. They would tell us the stories of their successes as well as their failures. They would tell us about precarious turning points that changed the way they did life and ministry. They would relay the stories that taught them what was important. In short, they would tell us about the events God used to establish their DNA as a church trying their best to follow Jesus and his mission.

How can I be so sure? Because that is exactly what Luke did.

Rather than outlining ecclesiological doctrines or polished plans for ministry success, Luke told us about

---

1   Robert Quinn, *Deep Change*. Jossey-Bass, 1996. p. 83.

the moments that formed the core of their DNA as the church—our DNA. Think about it: the book of Acts spans three decades. It references territory from the Eastern Mediterranean, the Horn of Africa, and across the Roman Empire. Despite its scope and seminal importance, it contains relatively little detail. It is clearly not a comprehensive history of the first century church. So, we have to wonder, how did Luke choose what he would include and what he would leave on the cutting room floor?

I submit that under the direction of the Holy Spirit, Luke chose to write about the critical events in the gestational process that formed the church. He told us what they learned about being the Body of Christ and the circumstances in which they learned it. He showed us not only how Jesus continued to reach the world through his people, but also how he continued shaping his people to reach that world.

And, that may be the genius of the book of Acts. Rather than telling us this is THE way and that we should copy what they did, Luke reveals the DNA that would show us how to thrive in any culture, in any context, at any time. The book of Acts is not a book of methods to be replicated, but a book whose stories tell us how we were made and what we were made for. It is time to stop asking how we can get back to the way they did things in the early church. It is time to start paying attention to the missiology[2] and ecclesiology[3] embedded in the stories of their journey.

---

2   Missiology refers to the research, theology, and best practice of Christian missions. For a fuller definition and description see the essay of Robert Priest at http://www.missiologymatters.com, Mar 7, 2012.

3   Ecclesiology is the technical term for the body of theology and study regarding the Church.

Luke wrote for us. He did not simply write history nor did he write a paint-by-numbers guide for other generations to follow. But, he did capture for all time the critical events that shaped the church of the first century for revolutionary impact. He shows us our DNA and, in so doing, shows us the keys to unleashing our revolutionary potential in the twenty-first century.

A Revolutionary Community

Let's admit it. This revolutionary movement called the church is an anomaly. Both organism and organization, the church is a community of broken people who also serve as the delivery system for the hope of the world. While profoundly human, we are simultaneously a people not of this world. There is a prophetic nature to who we are and the way we operate. God intends for the world around us to consider a new way of life when they look at the church. The very nature of how we were meant to do life and mission together makes a prophetic statement that interrupts the self-absorbed conversations of the world around us.

If the task of forming the life of the church had been left to our human nature, we would have created a very different institution. We would have crafted mechanisms to maximize comfort, safety, and security in a scary world. We would have placed power in the hands of a few and worried more about how they might serve us than how we might serve the poor. Then having put it all in place, we would spend our energies preserving the status quo rather than giving ourselves away. It is the way of organizations.

While the church is certainly a community of unvarnished humanity, God formed us in a way that releases his glory. At every turning point in the journey of this young congregation, the Spirit of God directed them in ways that run contrary to our human inclinations. The resulting counterintuitive community is not what we would have created, but is exactly what we are created for.

It is no surprise that words like awe, fear, amazement, and wonder were used to describe public reaction to this early community of Christ-followers. The things accomplished by these ordinary, unschooled men and women stunned all who observed them. Social elites of power and position felt threatened by their inability to explain away or thwart this growing movement.

In contrast, the Western church of the twentieth century became an icon of mainstream culture. Rather than a prophetic voice to our culture, we became a force to sustain social and cultural equilibrium. Mom, apple pie, and the church were supposed to go hand in hand. I wonder if some of our current angst about the state of the church flows more from concern over cultural and economic changes that marginalize us, than from our effectiveness at bringing the hope of the Gospel to a lost and broken world.

It is time to reintroduce a word into the operational lexicon and expectations of the church: *revolutionary*. Not revolutionary in the sense that we are here to destroy, but in the sense that the way we live, as well as the words we preach, ought to serve as a revolutionary invitation and influence for the kingdom. The community of Christ-followers called the church was wired to operate in our world in a manner that is life-givingly countercultural. We are citizens of another kingdom. We should be a people of hope who turn the world upside down as a normal course of business.

The notion of the church as a revolutionary force seems pretty far-fetched today. We are accustomed to a seat at the table of culture, to staid and sturdy buildings, to predictable schedules and gatherings, to tax benefits, to cultural holidays that coincide with the liturgical calendar, and to the personal benefits of extensive pastoral care systems.

When was the last Monday morning you showed up at work and told a co-worker you'd spent time over the weekend with a group of revolutionaries? How often do you think of your church as a radical outfit? Is it not more common that our mental picture of the church is one of a safe, steady, polite organization—one to be counted on as a bastion of stability in a swirling climate of change? It seems that our typical thoughts of the church are far removed from anything remotely "revolutionary."

Don't get me wrong. The church as a community should be a safe place. It should be a haven where broken people can thrive without having to perform and without fear of judgment. We should be what Larry Crabb called *The Safest Place on Earth*. But, safety does not trump everything else. In fact, the tension of safety and risk-taking mission is one piece of the paradox that defines this revolutionary community. We were created to do life *and* mission *together*. We are a community that declares *and* demonstrates the hope of heaven in a world where hell is all too familiar.

The days of playing it safe are over. The day for reclaiming our birthright has arrived. It is time to rediscover the church for which we were made. It is time to rediscover the church that was made for the lost world around us. It is time to learn what Jesus meant when he said, "the kingdom of heaven has been forcefully advancing and forceful men lay hold of it."[4]

Welcome to the Conversation

If you are reading this book, I think it is safe to say that you long for something more. Perhaps you would choose a different word than "revolutionary" to describe the church. However, regardless of the word you would choose, smoldering in you is a hunger for the church that could be. I stand with you.

There is a growing global conversation about all that it means to be the church. I believe the Spirit of God is fanning the flame of fresh thought and pioneering courage regarding all that it means to be the people of Christ on the mission of Christ in a lost and broken world. He is inviting us to join him. I write this book as a contribution to that global conversation. My prayer is that it will catalyze more thought, more exploration, and more discoveries that flow directly out of the Scriptures. Every one of the strands of DNA Luke writes about speak directly into the conversations we are having.

You need to know that I write as one who is deeply passionate about the health and impact of the church in my generation. Christianity in North America—the land I call home—is on a significant decline. Our large churches grow primarily because Christians migrate to them from other churches. We are dying faster than we are reaching our

---

4   Matthew 11.12

growing population. The world around us not only perceives us as irrelevant, but we are now seen by many as part of the problem—in some cases, even as a pariah.

It is my privilege to work with pastors, churches, lay leaders, seminaries, and denominational executives across the United States and around the world. As a leader in a mission organization focused on developing leaders who will strengthen and start churches worldwide, I hear the cries of leaders' hearts. In those conversations, both private and public, I hear of a panic-driven search for anything that will stop the hemorrhaging. Whether trying to navigate the rapids of discontinuous change or trying to clear the fog of simplistic ministry solutions, we are in a struggle for the future of the church and its influence in the world.

Let me be clear, I am not a deconstructionist. I have no desire to attack the church in order to throw her out as a worthless relic. Quite the contrary. I am awestruck by the way God uses his people as a called-out community to carry on the very work of Jesus. I marvel at the ways God continually transforms those who come to him and deploys them right back into a broken world. I am stunned by the way imperfect people are formed into a redemptive community. Even as a rough-edged human entity, the church is God's primary delivery system of hope in the world.

This is why I marvel at what is recorded in the book of Acts. While we become mired in dialogues about methods and the traditions of the past hundred years, the first century church literally made it up as they went along. While we fight to hold onto familiar ways at all cost, there were at least eight times where this infant church had to start over, restructuring the way they "did church." They learned to be the church "on the job," with the mission of Jesus at stake, even though the rules of the game changed at every turn.

Their story is breathtaking.

And, in the nuances of their revolutionary journey, we discover the DNA of our own heritage. This DNA will release the revolutionary capacity of the church in our own day. It is the DNA of your church.

This book is meant to be a source of hope and insight. It is an invitation to freedom and newfound passion. It is not a book of methods or simple solutions and it is not a book of confining dogmas. I expect it will challenge some of your familiar paradigms and cause you moments of discomfort. It will poke at some traditional thinking and might even add to the destabilization you already feel. I invite you to dream of all that could be possible if we learned to live in alignment with what we saw God do in the first century.

If you are looking for simplistic solutions, I will disappoint you. For that matter, so will the book of Acts. If you are willing to look at a familiar story[5] with fresh eyes, you will find life-giving freedom, creativity, and courage to unleash the revolutionary potential in the church you call home.

Expect to find your story in theirs and as a result, expect to be surprised by what you find. Give yourself permission to rediscover the church, maybe for the first time.

---

5   I do not use the word "story" because I believe the record in the book of Acts is fictional in any way. Quite the contrary, I hold that what Luke wrote is true in every way. For the sake of this book, I choose to use the word story as a term that reflects the nature of an unfolding adventure of discovery. Luke is telling us their "story" in a way that allows us to enter into the narrative as it happens.

two

The Power of Mission

ROAMING the landscape of the American church is a growing tribe of people I am calling the Tribe of the Weary Faithful. They are men and women who desire to honor and follow Jesus. They attend church faithfully, they serve, they give, they rarely complain, and yet, inside they ache for something much more profound. They long to do more with their lives. They long for a compelling cause to live for and a community in which to live it out.

Convinced that the church is instrumental to God's plan, this Tribe of the Weary Faithful shows up week after week, nursing a smoldering hope that maybe this Sunday they will discover a secret that unlocks a God-sized life. Most weeks, they get back in the car to drive home a little disappointed and a little bored. Over time, this repetitive experience on the hamster wheel ferments into a soul-deep numbness, or worse, cynical disillusionment.

Gary Haugen, President and CEO of International Justice Mission, said it this way:

> At the end of the day we thought our Christian life would be more than this—somehow larger, more significant, more vivid, more glorious. But it's not. Driving to church on Sunday feels a bit like Groundhog Day, the movie where Bill Murray's character is forced to pathetically relive exactly the same day over and over again.[6]

What happened? Why is it that as followers of the greatest revolutionary who ever lived, "revolutionary" is the last word most people would use to describe us? To quote Haugen again, "following Christ was supposed to be a bold adventure of power and beauty and singular importance."[7]

I watch church leaders who are eager to breathe new life into their churches become embroiled in conversations about forms—ministry methods, styles, and curriculums— the visible components of our life together. We rename what we are already doing, we adopt different curriculums for our small groups, we shift meeting times or locations, we beef up our multimedia, and we rename our churches. Even when we agree on bold new initiatives, we bog down in committees fixated on micro-steps of incremental adjustment.

Rather than more incremental change to our methodologies, it is time for a big conversation about the heart of our mission. It is time to rediscover the revolutionary

---

6   Gary Haugen, *Just Courage*. InterVarsity Press, 2008. p. 25-26.

7   ibid. p. 26.

core of who we are and what we are about as the Body of Christ. People in our congregations ache to be part of a bigger story, a church that makes a revolutionary difference in the world around us.

The movie *Braveheart* became a worldwide blockbuster, not only because of its spectacle as an epic story, but because it portrayed a common longing for a cause worthy of our lives. In my own words, the resonant point of the movie is that without a cause worth dying for, we don't have a cause worth living for.

That cause? The redemptive agenda of Jesus that shapes our nature and mission as his people. At the center of who we are is a God-sized mission. It is so important that this is *the* starting point from which Luke told the story of the early church. The church we long for is not a pipe dream and the journey toward it begins with renewed clarity about the nature of our mission.

When Luke picked up his pen and started writing what we know as the book of Acts, he devoted page one to answering the question of what matters most. Luke opened the story by showing us that Jesus' final act before to his ascension was to declare our central priority as the people who bear his name. Jesus chose us to carry his message of hope and life and healing into a desperate world. He chose us to tell his story. He said, "Live…as my witness…[from here] to the ends of the earth and I will empower you through my Holy Spirit as you go."[8]

We are the agents of his redemptive plan.

---

8   A slight paraphrase of Acts 1.6-8

The Backstory

In order to fully appreciate the weight of Jesus' words that day, we need to step into the backstory surrounding the events we read about in Acts 1.

Put yourself in the shoes of Jesus' disciples. For three years you traveled the length and breadth of the country as a tight-knit group. You spent time in homes of the rich and powerful and you spent time in the presence of lepers and outcasts. You heard the words of God spoken in real time. You saw miracles. You cast out demons. Everything about your life, your relationships, your interests, and your destiny changed during these years with Jesus.

On one Friday, forty days ago all of it collapsed. You witnessed the trauma and horrors of Jesus' crucifixion firsthand. You spent the weekend hiding while the nation spent it celebrating. You feared that at any moment, a knock on the door would mean you were next. Though the city teemed with crowds, you hid in the shadows whispering. And then, Sunday happened. The resurrection changed everything.

Now, in the past few days you and the other close followers of Jesus sense something is up. No one can put their finger on it, but tentative conversations abound. In the countenance and conversations of Jesus, it is clear that something is about to change, again. Then while sharing a meal, Jesus starts speaking about waiting in Jerusalem, the promised gift, and being baptized by the Holy Spirit.[9]

---

9   See Acts 1:3-6

Two thousand years later, all of us know that the Ascension was about to take place. Our familiarity with basic New Testament history makes it nearly impossible to hear the events of Scripture with fresh ears. For those disciples on that day, there were no clues about what lay ahead. Everything happened in real time with life-altering consequences.

Can you imagine the ambiguity they felt? The tension? The wonderment? Their anticipation paints the backdrop to a pregnant question:

> Lord, are you at this time going to restore the kingdom to Israel?[10]

In first century Israel, Messianic hope permeated the culture. The dream of expelling Roman rule and installing a theocratic government in Jerusalem throbbed in the soul of Jewish thought. So, on the surface this question sounds just like the hope of all Israel. If Jesus answered by saying, "yes," it would announce the fulfillment of Israel's religious and nationalistic hopes.

I want to suggest there was a question behind their question.[11] The destiny of Israel was not the only thing on the minds of the disciples. This was personal. After three years on the road, sleeping in strange places night after night, depending on others for food and money, and being harassed

---

10 Acts 1:6

11 The Messianic nature and promise embedded in this question deserves extended study. However, for the purposes of this book, I will leave that work to others and focus instead on the issues behind this request.

by the religious elite of Israel, could it be the disciples of Jesus longed to settle down?

Is it not reasonable to wonder if nomadic life was growing a little thin? Think about it. If Jesus were to set up his rule and reign in Jerusalem, they could settle down, sleep in their own beds every night, raise families, build homes, grow gardens, and finally get some real respect.

I can imagine a myriad of unspoken thoughts running through the minds of these disciples:

> *"What a great idea! Jesus, if you would set up shop and rule from Jerusalem, everyone would know where to find you."*

> *"We could avoid wasting so much time traveling and could devote more time to the ministry."*

> *"We could build classrooms for teaching your followers the lessons you have taught us."*

> *"We could hold big events in the large amphitheaters where acoustics are much easier to control than random hillsides by the sea."*

> *"Imagine the spectacular celebrations we could pull off at Christmas and Easter."*

All right, maybe I am pushing it, but consider Jesus' response. On the surface, their question sounds like the Messianic hope of all Israel. But, Jesus' reply shows us he picked up on the deeper implications of what they were asking. The very nature of what it means to follow him—the heart and mission of the church—will be implicated by his reply. His answer seems out of context, unless he heard a deeper question behind the question.

> You will receive power when the Holy Spirit comes on you; and you will be my witnesses in Jerusalem, and in all Judea and Samaria, and to the ends of the earth.[12]

In my paraphrase of the conversation, the disciples asked, "Jesus, can we finally set up shop in Jerusalem?" Jesus replied, "No. I did not call you to be a set-up-shop people. You are a sent people. I did not call you to be a community that waits for the world to come to you. You are to be a band of witnesses going to the world all around you—a community of people on mission. Just as I invited you to come and follow me a long time ago, I am sending you with my Spirit as witnesses into this world that I love."

Three Shifts in Our Posture

The conversation between Jesus and his followers in Acts 1:6-8 happens so fast that we can easily miss the repercussions of what he said. In that one statement, Jesus interrupts a great deal of the way we think and talk about the church and the Christian life. He marked us as people called to live outside our cloistered walls of safety and in redemptive relationships with those who surround us. We were never intended to fortress-up, withdrawing from a big bad hostile world. We were rescued to become rescuers.

---

12 Acts 1.8

However, there is more to living out this life than embracing well-intended words. This first strand of our DNA—the heart of our mission—has provocative implications for us. In practical terms, it calls for at least three major shifts in our posture as the church. It shapes the way we think, the priorities by which we live, and the way we relate to the world around us.

Shift #1: *From* Witness*ing to* Witness*es*

We start with a head-on collision over language. Quite frankly, I think this declaration of Jesus is hard for most of us to get excited about because the word "witnesses" makes us cringe. For many, maybe most, churched folks in the twenty-first century, the word "witnesses" comes loaded with baggage. Even though Jesus used it to define our mission, until we get past our resistance to the term itself, we will struggle to embrace the life he envisioned when he said it.

At some point in recent decades, witnessing came to mean that confrontational style of evangelism where well-meaning people accost strangers at the mall or a park or by going door-to-door in order to present them with the "plan of salvation." I don't criticize the motives or the gifting of the few who may see fruit this way, but, as a general rule, this approach yields little results and appeals to very few. It is relationally and culturally invasive at best. Worse, it reduces our relationship with people who need to know the transformational hope of the Good News into a transactional event. Witnessing like this means cold-calling among strangers rather than storytelling among friends. It replicates the experience we have when uninvited salespeople or members of a cult come knocking on our door.

What if instead of drudgery and discomfort, Jesus was inviting us into a way of life that was life-giving? What if witnessing his way was creative, adventurous, and natural? What if being a witness was more about telling our story than regurgitating a canned presentation? The actual word Jesus used is really quite simple. It is the word we would use to describe an eyewitness. An eyewitness has a fairly simple task. They are not responsible to persuade. They only need to tell the story of what they saw or experienced firsthand. In truth, being a witness is not complicated.

By the way, did you notice Jesus said *be* my witnesses and not *do* witnessing? It is subtle, but significant. Being witnesses to the Savior has as much to do with the way we live and love among broken people as it does with what we say. It is time to think beyond witnessing as a project or an event and begin to embrace all it means to be a witness as a way of life. Being a witness is a holistic approach that includes everything we do to demonstrate and declare the Good News.

At the end of the age, God's work of redemption will lead to the re-creation of a new heaven and a new earth— redeeming all the ravages of hell—to establish his kingdom in full. Look around. As a starting point, just ask yourself, what are all the things you see that God will set right when he creates a new heaven and new earth? If God cares about them in the future, he cares about them in the present. We are surrounded by opportunities to be good news and demonstrate the hope of heaven by addressing the ravages of hell right now. So, as a starting point, choose to do something about one of them now. Do what Joe Aldrich described more than 30 years ago: learn to play the music of the Gospel in order to create a desire for the words of the Gospel.[13]

SHIFT #2: *FROM MEMBERS TO MISSIONARIES*

"It's not about you."[14]

Rick Warren's opening line is one of the most profound statements in his book, *The Purpose Driven Life*. However, on a day-to-day and down-to-earth basis, this is not the way we think about the church from the perspective of the pew. We expect the church to minister to us. None of us would demand that our personal preferences should rule the day in our churches, but most of us expect our preferences to be given due consideration. We even talk about "shopping for a church" as if church was a commodity to be selected, acquired, and consumed.

This is how members think. Membership is about rights and privileges. It is about joining and belonging. Members of an organization focus on the goods and services they receive in exchange for their membership. They demand a voice in where things are going and choose leaders who represent their needs and opinions. If, or when, the organization ceases to go the way they desire, they vote with their feet. So, no surprise, the natural inclination of any organization is to focus on gaining, keeping, and satisfying its members.

---

13   Joe Aldrich made this observation in his book, *Lifestyle Evangelism*. Multnomah Press, 1981.

14   Rick Warren, *The Purpose Driven Life*. Zondervan, 2002. p. 17.

And, this is exactly what makes the first strand of our DNA so revolutionary.

We were commissioned as ambassadors of reconciliation who bring grace and truth to a fallen world. We are God's primary delivery system of hope. We are witnesses. It is a mission that is bigger than any of us.

The word for people who live on mission? Missionaries.

But this paradigm shift creates real tension. In the vernacular of typical religious thought, "missionaries" are people who don't live normal lives with normal jobs in the normal world. They move somewhere far away to reach people who are not like us—often someplace we deem poor or exotic or dangerous. Contemporary Christian culture operates on the assumption that the church exists to care for us and missionaries exist to care for "them."

It is time to repatriate the concept of missionary. That is, bring it back home and weave the notion of a missionary life into our understanding of the ordinary Christian life to be lived out every day. We have a missionary God who called us to follow him on his mission in a lost and broken world. To join him on mission is to be a missionary. Yes, some "missionaries" will be apostolically gifted and called to extend the Gospel in cross-cultural contexts. But, every Christ-follower is called to a missionary life. The normal life for ordinary followers of Jesus is to live as missionaries in their everyday lives. And, as a result, every local church is a missionary outpost—a community of Christians on mission together.

Think about it this way. Imagine that the people of your church, whether 50 or 5,000, were a missionary band intentionally deployed into your city in order to reach it for Christ? Think about it in the same way that a team of missionaries would be sent to a place like Papua New Guinea. If you viewed your assignment to your community in this way, how would it change the way you live as a church?

I am sure by this point you feel the tension of the paradox. Isn't the church supposed to be a nurturing, caring community that helps people grow? Isn't it supposed to be about us, the people who are already gathered? After all, the Epistles are filled with "one another" passages. We are supposed to love one another.

The answer to the tension is yes. Yes, to both. The very nature of a paradox means that both things are true. At the same time, when push comes to shove, something comes first. Luke will tell us a great deal more about life within the Body of Christ as we continue in Acts, but at the end of the day, it is not enough to be a loving community. First and foremost, we are eyewitnesses to the answer for all mankind.

Learning to think and live like missionaries provokes a significant shift in the way we have grown accustomed to life in the church, but it does something else, too. In a world that is all about "me," people who are all about others stand out. Living as a community of missionaries who prioritize their attention on others creates a revolutionary and prophetic posture that interrupts the pointlessness of a self-centered and self-absorbed world.

SHIFT #3: *FROM ATTRACTION TO INCARNATION*

I think it would be safe to describe the ministry posture of the American church during the last half of the twentieth century as the *Field of Dreams* model. That is, "if we build it, they will come." We did build it and, for a long time, they did come. We worked hard to provide quality services, meaningful sermons, and special events that people who don't follow Christ might be drawn to. We urged our members to invite unchurched friends to special events and programs held on the church campus. The life of the congregation orbited around the building and we hoped other people would find what we did there to be attractive.

Can we be honest? Have you noticed a shrinking number of people respond to these efforts who are not already followers of Christ? These strategies worked for quite a while, but our culture has changed. I don't fault the motives of churches that took this approach. I spent many years as a pastor working hard to design attractive ways of exposing others to who we are and to the Savior we serve. But I am suggesting that as a missiologically effective strategy for reaching a *lost* world, this attractional approach is just not working well anymore. The mandate of Acts 1.8 declares that our fundamental nature demands an incarnational approach. Rather than waiting for people to come to us, we are witnesses *sent* to them.

The time has come for us to look one another in the eye and admit that the world at our doorstep is staying away from the church *on purpose*. They avoid us intentionally. People in our neighborhoods do not sit down for dinner on Sunday evening surprised by regret because they forgot to go to church again. Increasingly, this post-Christian culture perceives the church as more than irrelevant. We are often seen as part of the problem. Our repeated efforts to gain people's attention and invite them to what we do is only turning up the volume for people who don't want to listen anymore.

An attractional posture means trying to get people to come to us. It assumes some level of hunger to know God *and* a level of trust in us. An incarnational posture means building bridges to them. Incarnation means living among, engaged in relationship with, and tolerating the messiness of life with broken people. It means walking at the speed of others' spiritual interest as we earn the right to be heard.

I am not arguing for throwing the baby out with the bath water. There is no need for either/or thinking—as in, either attractional or incarnational. Enough residual Gospel awareness exists that a small portion of the population will come to us when they are ready. We should continue to prepare for them. We should strive to do things well. We should create safe places for those who are beginning to seek Christ. However, because our church culture is so entrenched in an attractional way of life, achieving the balance of both/and will call for disproportionate effort. Making the shift to an incarnational posture will call for enormous energy and intentionality. When a people and/or an organization are accustomed to doings one way, new behavior and new priorities will feel foreign for some time. It will take deliberate attention over an extended period of time before living and thinking incarnationally becomes second nature.

Jesus modeled this life for us. "The Word became flesh and dwelled among us full of grace and truth."[15] "He did not consider equality with God a thing to be grasped, but made

---

15 John 1.14

himself nothing, taking the very nature of a servant."[16] As his followers, his mission and his method have been entrusted to us. They are actually in our DNA.

The Life We Long For

We are drawn to the book of Acts because in it we find a wholly different kind of church life and impact—the revolutionary life we long for. The pathway to that life, as a church, begins by aligning our congregation with the DNA of our mission as witnesses. Far more than a life-draining and duty-driven mandate, alignment with our mission unlocks the vibrant life for which we were made. Our mission as witnesses means living into the global-eternal mission of God. It is a larger-than-life reason for everything we do. This is the starting point of a new day for that Tribe of the Weary Faithful.

When a local congregation spends its energies giving itself away to the people and needs around them, they discover the life they longed for all along. God is alive and active beyond the walls of our buildings and when we sacrificially engage with people in that lost and broken world, we discover him more fully than we could have ever predicted. On the contrary, when congregational life narrows to meeting our needs, we get seduced into endless arguments about preferences, traditions, and trivial matters of personal comfort.

This is the upside down, inside out paradox of the kingdom we see throughout the Scriptures. In giving you

16 Philippians 2.6-7

receive. If you want to be first, be last. If you want to become great, become the servant of all. If you want to find your life, give it away. If you want to know Christ, deny yourself, take up your cross, and follow him.

To be the church Jesus commissioned is to be first and foremost a community of people who live as witnesses. It is not about what we are going to get, it is about everything we have to give. It is not about those who are already in the house, it is about those outside the walls. It is about living in relationship with others as witnesses who tell the story of Jesus, in word and in deed. It is about following Jesus and aligning everything we do with his mission. And, when we live this way, we find that our souls thrive, our relationships grow deeper, our gatherings take on new life, and the number of disciples increases.

When we live this way, joy becomes the norm. Boredom becomes a thing of the past. Pettiness fades where there is meaning and purpose and adventure and risk. Sacrifice leads to health. We stop fighting over differing opinions and start fighting to find ways to reach the world at our front door. It is the type of revolutionary movement for which it is worth giving our lives. After all, the story we are part of—the story we have to tell—is about the greatest leader who ever lived, the hope of all mankind.

Everything that follows in the book of Acts builds upon and helps us live out this mission to the world. Every strand of our DNA as the Body of Christ is linked to and inseparable from this starting point. The question for us is whether this mission as his witnesses lives at the center of everything we do.

three

Getting the Who Right

THERE is no decision making process of greater strategic importance or with more far reaching implications than that of leadership selection. Leaders are game changers.

Local churches face the challenge of leadership selection on a regular basis. Typically, some form of appointment or nominating process happens every year where churches select new elders, deacons, board members, and other types of ministry leaders. Every once in a while they face the daunting assignment of calling a new senior pastor or key pastoral staff member. The question to be asked in all of those situations is, what are the absolutely essential criteria that leaders in the church need to meet regardless of their role?

Imagine that late one evening, you get a phone call. On the other end of the line, your elder board chairman tells you that your pastor just accepted a position at another church and will be going public with the announcement of his plans this Sunday. Your chairman asks you to consider leading the pastoral search team. He says you will not need to do any work on it this week, he just wants to put a few transitional pieces in place before the public announcement is made. Now you lie in bed with your eyes wide open, unable to stop the torrent of thoughts racing through your mind.

Can you picture the situation? Can you imagine the conversation in your head? What questions would you be asking? What challenges would you face? What criteria come to mind immediately regarding what matters most in a potential new pastor?

In theory, we recognize that pastors are only human, but in truth, it is easy to put them on a pedestal. None of us expects blue tights, a red cape, and funky red boots, but our standards for a pastor hover near the superhero category. We want to find a pastor who has the ...

- spiritual depth of Brother Lawrence
- compassion of Mother Teresa
- communication skills of Francis Chan
- theological prowess of Tim Keller
- organizational genius of Jim Collins
- financial savvy of Dave Ramsay
- evangelistic impact of Billy Graham or Bill Bright
- leadership horsepower of Bill Hybels
- family values of Dennis Rainey
- sage-like wisdom of Yoda

Factors magnified by the process of selecting a new pastor are only slightly reduced when it comes to leadership selection and appointment on other levels in the church. I work with ministry leaders every day. I watch them wear themselves out trying to satisfy the super-human standards of our modern era. I hear the stories of conflicting expectations and congregational frustration. We have become a culture of armchair quarterbacks skilled in the art of second-guessing those who lead us. It should not be that way.

Leadership within the Body of Christ should be a different experience than that of our culture. It should be life-giving rather than soul-starving. If we are a church who embodies the Good News, then serving as a leader in any arena of church life should be an experience of good news.

Luke starts us on a journey to a better way by bringing our attention to what matters most regarding ministry leaders. In fact, the same criteria that guide leadership selection are the building blocks for healthier leadership execution. The question is not what are all the things that matter when it comes to leadership, but what are the few things that matter most. Beyond particular skills, experiences, and gifting, what lies at the center of life for a leader that supersedes everything else we might be tempted to list as important?

The Rabbi is Gone

The safety net of the Rabbi's presence was gone. The Ascension of Jesus created the first organizational transition in the church. The loss of a loved senior pastor or founding church planter can be traumatic, but it doesn't hold a candle to what the early church faced at Jesus' ascension. Jesus was the heart, the leader, the embodiment of the cause, the one they had given up everything to follow. Jesus was not only the founding leader of the movement—he was the movement.

In Jesus' absence, questions of leadership succession become immediately critical. What would be the best way forward? Should one person take Jesus' place? Should the inner circle of Peter, James, and John form a leadership triad? Should the eleven lead as a team since no one person could ever replace Jesus? Who and how should they make all these decisions? The early church was in uncharted territory. No person or group had ever chosen a leader for a role in the church prior to this moment.

Suspend what you know about the rest of the story and consider what they were feeling. The eleven apostles learned about leadership from the only perfect leader the world has ever known. Can you imagine how intimidating it must have been to consider trying to fill *his* shoes? They were now the leaders of the movement for which he gave his life. Their actions and decisions would forever shape the future of his church. They had walked with the Messiah and knew better than anyone how wide the gap was between who they were and who he was. The weight of the world—in an appropriate sense—was on their shoulders.

Cut to the scene in the upper room. We know that Jesus ascended to heaven forty days after his resurrection and we know that the Day of Pentecost is fifty days after Passover, but apart from that little detail is known regarding what took place during that ten-day gap. Luke picks up the narrative with what happened at the point when Peter made a formal recommendation to replace Judas. The effect of Luke's writing style is to focus all of our attention on the criteria of a new leader, not on the process that determined that criteria. In short, Luke points the spotlight on what matters most for those who would be leaders in the body and mission of Christ.

By contrast, when local churches seek to appoint key leaders, there are often a swirling number of criteria vying for congregational attention. The most troublesome of these moments comes when it is time to fill governing board roles. Ambiguity over what really matters most gives way to expediency. It is not uncommon at all for churches to appoint leaders based on their executive experience, political influence in the congregation, longevity as a member, or the size of their bank account. However, leadership is about influence and influence flows out of who we are.

What Peter says cuts away the fog of leadership complexity. While pastoral search committees create multi-page documents that detail church priorities and extensive job descriptions, Luke tells us that they focused on three things that qualify a leader. Think about it. Peter narrowed the entire realm of reasonable leadership competencies and responsibilities to three essentials[17] that define what matters most in leaders of the church.

1. A track record of intimacy with Jesus
2. A life of witness
3. A commitment to live and lead in community

---

17 These three criteria are listed in Acts 1.21-22. The full upper room conversation is recorded in Acts 1.15-26.

1. A Track Record of Intimacy with Jesus

Peter's exact words were, "Choose one of the men who have been with us the whole time the Lord Jesus went in and out among us."[18] They needed someone who had been with Jesus, who can speak out of his own experience, who has a personal story to tell. In that moment, the apostolic assignment called for firsthand witnesses to the events, teaching, miracles, and resurrection of Jesus. In principle, this criteria remains unchanged.

The preeminent quality for leadership in the church is someone whose life is anchored in sustained communion with the Savior. These are leaders who walk with Jesus in the trenches of daily life. They have been transformed by their relationship with Jesus and will naturally long for others to know what they have experienced. Leaders like this model what Jesus meant when he called us to abide in Him.[19] Their lives echo the evidence of the greatest commandment, that we love the Lord our God with all our heart and soul and mind.[20]

It is so very tempting to try and build a list of essential behaviors that would serve as a benchmark to measure the validity of someone's daily relationship with Jesus. Yes, we would expect to find the practice of classic spiritual disciplines, but a report card does not equal a relationship. This is about the pattern of a life as much as it is about the specific practices of that life. The result is that the presence

---

18 Acts 1.21

19 John 15

20 Matthew 22.37

of Jesus in their life is unmistakable. We should be able to say about the leaders of a church what was said about Peter and John: "they were astonished and they took note that these men had been with Jesus."[21]

Think of it this way. Imagine you had a dozen men and women in their twenties in your home one evening. You were engaged in a conversation about the cynicism of a generation who wonders where authentic and passionate followers of Jesus are to be found. If you could invite them to shadow the leaders of your church and know that they will discover the authentic followers of Jesus they seek, then you know your leaders are the right stuff. Leaders who meet this first criteria are those who would be able to humbly say, "Come follow my example as I follow the example of Christ."[22]

2. A Life of Witness

Peter's declaration in the upper room should not really come as a surprise. If the central strand of our DNA defines our mission with mandate to be witnesses, then it makes perfect sense that our leaders should embody that mission. If we are all to be witnesses, leaders need to model the life of a witness. People on mission require leaders on mission. A missionary movement needs missionary leaders. This revolutionary entity called the church needs leaders who model a life of engagement in a lost world and this way of life is of greater importance than any skill or experience they bring to the conference room.

---

21 Acts 4.13

22 1 Corinthians 11.1

Consider the ripple effect that flows from the type of people we place in positions of leadership. Leaders influence the culture and priorities of the entire congregation by the pattern of their lives. Leaders who live a life of witness see the implications of every board decision differently than those who don't. They view money and buildings and pastoral staff differently. Leaders who are living as witnesses mentor others differently. Leaders who are not living as active witnesses of Jesus can repeat the rhetoric, but they cannot invite others to join them in a life of mission. Our DNA calls for leaders who lead by example and invite others to come join them.

It is hard to change the rules in the middle of the game. If leaders are selected for other qualities, but lack the track record of someone who is actively engaged as a witness, it is tough to come back later and expect a new baseline of behavior.

This standard, that leaders live as witnesses, has an impact on our fundamental understanding of what it means to live as a follower of Christ. Leaders are models, examples of the life we want emulated. This does not mean that they are perfect, but it does interrupt the prevalent notion in Western Christianity that it is possible to get to full maturity in Christ apart from a life on mission to the world around us. We cannot live fully as followers of Jesus inside the walls of the church, be they literal or social-relational walls. To follow Jesus is to follow him into relationship with people that need to meet him.

Leaders reproduce themselves. Jesus told us, "Everyone, who is fully trained, will be like his teacher."[23] I submit that in

---

23 Luke 6.40

a parallel way, when a congregation has been fully trained it will be like its leaders. If church leaders spend all their time running the machine, we should not be surprised when our best people spend all of their available time in the programs of the church and have no time or energy left for engaging a lost world. We should not be surprised when everyone burns out simply trying to keep up with an overly booked schedule of church-centric activities.

But, this is about much more than getting it right. The implication of this leadership DNA offers hope for the bored and the exhausted leader. Leadership should be an adventure into the larger mission of the church in the world. Personal and shared participation in that mission is a place of life-giving joy. Engaging in the work of redeeming the world is the antidote to institutionalism. A great many godly men and women said yes to serving in positions of ministry leadership out of a deep desire to see the world changed, only to be seduced into drudgery. When an institutional mindset takes over—a focus on keeping things running well, safe, and under control—they experience a slow erosion in their souls. They begin to lose enthusiasm, creativity, risk, and hope.

Like so many aspects of following Christ, there is a leadership paradox here, too. Leading a church into mission in a complex world demands leadership and organizational competency. At the same time, if we get everything right about running a great organization, but fail to be primarily about living in redemptive relationships with a lost and broken world, we got it wrong. If leaders only focus on running the church well, it should come as no surprise that the life our people aspire to is devoid of a priority for engaging lost people.

When Peter stood up during that upper room meeting, he outlined an approach to church leadership that feels different than the norm of our day. It is simple. It is life-giving. It is an extension of our mission. The role of leaders is to lead the way, showing all of us how to live a life of mission that flows out of intimacy with Jesus. The church is unleashed to focus on reaching those beyond our walls when its leaders focus on living in relationship with them. And, by the way, contrary to our individualized approaches in Western culture, leaders were not meant to pull it off alone.

3. Commitment to Live and Lead in Community

It could be argued that the American cowboy—at least the caricature of the cowboy—is the quintessential icon of American culture. There he sits on his chestnut brown horse, well-traveled leather jacket, coiled rope slung over the horn of his saddle, with rugged peaks in the background, while the setting sun paints the sky. He looks to be the master of life in a simpler era. Self-sufficient, relationally non-entangled, emotionally uncomplicated, and without any commitments tying him down, he can change his plans and chase the horizon at any time. Pipe in a little inspiring music and the whole scene feels rather inviting. The problem is, this is airbrushed fiction. It is the quintessential picture of our cultural captivity to American individualism.

Peter's third criteria interrupts this kind of individualism by calling for leaders who are committed to leading and living interdependently. Leadership in the Body of Christ is a matter of "we," not "I."[24]

The point is made so quickly and so subtly it can easily get missed. The right leader "…must become a witness *with us* of [Jesus'] resurrection."[25] Did you catch it? He said, this new leader must become a witness *together with us*. You can almost sense that in that day, the pattern of leading together went without saying. But, in the Western world of the twenty-first century, we are so accustomed to thinking of leaders as great individuals we need to deliberately pause to reflect on all that he meant. Leaders do not operate as solo stars, but as collaborative partners. This criteria calls for more than parallel play, it dictates that leaders work in community and in concert together. As a matter of fact, you see this commitment played out on the very next page of Scripture. On the day of Pentecost it says that all twelve *stood up together* to address the crowd.[26]

American superhero notions of leadership are all about the individual, but this third criteria for leadership in the Body of Christ calls for those who will work together. No single leader has all the spiritual gifts. No individual has a corner on godly wisdom. None of us has the only pipeline to the guidance of the Spirit. The cumulative interaction and contributions of a team of leaders releases the fullness of Jesus' leadership through the Spirit. The point is, in the Body of Christ, a leadership team operates as a microcosm

---

24 One of my colleagues, Paul Ford, recently published the book, *Moving from I to We: Recovering the Biblical Vision for Stewarding the Church.* NavPress, 2013.

25 Acts 1.22, italics added

26 Acts 2.14

of the community life you long for throughout the whole church. They model unity around mission. They demonstrate the rhythms and complementary giftedness that make the Body of Christ so dynamic. If you want to see where the life of your congregation is headed, look at the way your leaders work together.

When leaders in the Body of Christ lead out of community like this, we discover a prophetic voice. Living and leading interdependently breaks the bonds of our cultural captivity to rugged individualism. We emasculate the cult of leadership superstars when a plurality of leaders shares the spotlight. Our Western culture treasures things and uses people, but interdependent leaders break that mold. When you care more about people than what they produce, when you defang the cult of personality-driven leadership, when you share authority together, when you delight in the contributions of others, and when you confront the illusion of self-sufficiency, your actions declare that someone else reigns here.

Implications for Leadership Development

I can imagine that thinking about these criteria as the baseline for leadership selection could create some real tension in your church. What if you need to appoint new ministry leaders, but cannot find enough who are living strong in all three areas? What if you already are having trouble finding enough leaders? Resolving this tension can only be accomplished three ways. One, you compromise on the standards of leadership. Two, you become intentional about developing the leaders you need. Or, three, you just wait and hope that leaders like this move to your church, having been developed by someone else somewhere else. I think the second option is the only real choice.

If the kind of leaders we need are those who walk deeply with Jesus, live a life of holistic witness, and practice deep-seated commitment to life in community, then these three themes define the most important components of our leadership development strategy. To say it another way, attention to developing leaders is a seamless addition to our efforts at making and forming disciples of Jesus. These three qualities define the center of the normal Christian life and therefore, they need to be central to way we shape leaders.

Let me offer two insights as a framework for building a healthy leader development strategy. The first is to take a hands-on approach rather than an academic one. Leaders are not developed by reading books or covering concepts in a classroom. It's not that structured information and fresh learning do not matter. But, new learning that is anchored in personal experience brings about lasting impact. Think on-the-job training. Leaders are formed best when they have the chance to act and then reflect on their experience in the context of supportive relationships. This is what Jesus did with his disciples over and over and over.

The second insight is that although we have been talking about leading in community as the third criteria for a leader, it is probably the first component to be established when it comes to their development. Build a mutually interdependent learning community where leaders contribute to one another's personal growth and development. Don't ignore issues of ministry philosophy and organizational competency, but put primary attention on what you put into practice together. Engage in spiritually forming disciplines, get out of the room and do ministry together, and all along the way, talk about it. Adults learn best through action combined with reflection.

Apply this pattern to the way you invest in the ongoing development of existing leaders. Build attention to these three priorities into the normal practice of your life as a leadership team. Whether you are on the elder board, pastoral staff, or the leadership team over children's ministries, interrupt your fixation on tasks and decisions and devote significant chunks of time to these three formational practices. Frame your life as a community of leaders around the qualities you long to see commonplace in your church. Spend extended time in spiritually forming disciplines, discovering the easy yoke of Jesus when it comes to the responsibilities you carry. Get away from the conference room together and engage in ministry outside your church walls. Become the church in microcosm as you invest in one another's life and leadership development.

And, here's the kicker. If the leadership teams of your church became developmental environments like this, they would simultaneously serve as ideal apprenticing environments for emerging and potential new leaders. You would not need to create separate training programs for leaders. Every leadership team would become a developmental powerhouse. If at some point you decide to supplement what takes place among your different ministry teams for the sake of advanced training for developing leaders, keep the same pattern in place. Devote as much time to cultivating deeper intimacy with Christ and to engaging the world "out there" as you do to any focused training for leadership "in here."

I have begun hearing about a few places where senior leadership teams—pastoral staff and governing boards alike—have started getting out of the boardroom to do ministry together. One of my favorite stories is an elder board that went on a short-term mission trip together. By itself that move was bold and life-giving, but the thing that made it really powerful is that each of them brought one person they were discipling to follow Jesus more deeply. What made their experience so powerful was not simply that they traveled somewhere to do intensive ministry together. It was another step in how they had started living and leading differently, locally, every day.

You don't have to wait for the whole church or your whole leadership team to buy in. Take a look at your own life. Are you satisfied with what you see about the depth of these three core qualities? If God is shaping you as a leader of kingdom influence, then the place to get started is where you can take new ground in your own life. Who are a few people with whom you might form a learning community and with whom you could help one grow in the practices that fuel intimacy with Jesus and witness to a broken world?

The Shift in Action

A true story may be the best way to tie a bow around the implications of this chapter.

It was the fall of 1996 and the second afternoon of a two-day workshop I conducted for pastors and church leaders for one denomination in Saskatchewan, Canada. For nearly two days we had worked together on thoughts about how disciples, leaders, and churches are formed. We wrestled together over the ways they programmed the life of their local congregations. In so doing, the conclusions of our assessment revealed that their current practices mirrored those of the church throughout North America. (Allow me to name these conclusions in the first person. We can see ourselves in their situation.)

We discovered that nearly 100 percent of the organized programs in our churches focused on the work of member care: gathering, encouraging, and developing people who were already believers. While we give a nod to the priority of evangelism and to the need for engaging the brokenness of the world around us, it was primarily an intellectual acknowledgement. We lived with a Christian life overflowing with church activities and church people. We perpetuated a bubble of churched culture where we expected our leaders to serve us and maintain our comfortable patterns of life.

It was a tough conversation, but God was working to interrupt business as usual. The Spirit of God was calling us to a new normal, to a life where the norm for every disciple meant a life of disciplemaking. To be a follower of Jesus means we seek to develop other followers from the harvest and for the harvest. And, to be a leader in the church of Jesus is to model that disciplemaking life.

Finally, at a climactic point during our last afternoon, the denominational leader for the group stood up to address his people. He told them of his deep longing to live a life where relationship with people who don't follow Christ was commonplace. He ached for the freedom to protect his schedule so that he might be free to go places and do things with his neighbors and friends. Then, with a level of vulnerability rarely seen in such gatherings, he said, "I fear that a firestorm would erupt if I was unavailable to respond to a request from one of our churches because I was spending time with a non-believing friend."

Speaking directly to his pastors and their congregational leaders, he continued, "If I started making time to be with people who don't know Jesus on a regular basis, to engage in the needs of my community, to become involved with the poor and marginalized, your churches wouldn't understand. You expect that I am always on call, that I will always answer the phone, and that I will drop everything in order to be available to you at every moment of the day."

And with that admission, the rest of our training plans went out the window. Here was the leader of this whole group, eager to live the pattern Peter held up as the heart of leadership, afraid of the backlash if he did. The longing of this man changed the tenor of the day. His vulnerability in that moment immediately began to influence the priorities of the larger community of churches. We shifted our plans for the afternoon and went to work addressing the pathway for change—both for him and for the churches in the room. The transformation of a leader unleashes the impact of a church.

The challenge for all of us is to look closely at the people we appoint to roles of leadership and what we expect from them. There is no more powerful transformation than what happens when leaders start to live and lead according to the DNA discussed in that upper room. The role of a leader in the Body of Christ is fundamentally not about oiling and operating the treadmill of religious machinery. Peter gave us permission—even a mandate—to prioritize deeper relationship with Jesus, engagement with lost people, and the discipline to live this way as leaders in community together.

It is so simple.

But, it changes everything.

four

An Apprenticing Community

W^{HAT} do we do now?

It is a question we all ask from time to time. I am certain it was a question the apostles asked each other the morning after Pentecost.

A good friend of mine once told me about the way he dealt with puzzling ministry situations as a Senior Pastor. Steve's story went like this:

Whenever I faced a ministry challenge or found a program in the church not working well, I would call our denominational publishing group. They connected me to a resource specialist and I would describe our dilemma or desired goals. Invariably, the specialist recommended a new curriculum or program designed to meet our need. A few days later, the magic solution would be delivered to my door. I took those packages from our UPS driver and tore into them as if bold printing on the outside of the box read, "Problem Solved. Just add water and stir."[27]

Sure, we laugh at the notion that ministry and leadership could ever be as simple as "add water and stir," but our behavior says we believe otherwise. Pastors and church leaders race from conference to conference. We spend hours scouring the latest and greatest on Amazon.com. We try to replicate the current programming trends of growing churches. Our actions betray our belief that somewhere out there is a formula that will transform our church and fill our pews with members that tithe.

A few years back, a denominational executive in Kentucky told one of my colleagues that he was facing a new kind of trouble with his pastors. It seems that after attending one of Saddleback's Pastors' Conferences they would return home and step into the pulpit the next weekend wearing a Hawaiian shirt and shoes without socks. Somehow, the Cliff Notes™ application of what they took home from those good conferences was that California fashion is the secret to dynamic ministry. Who knew?

The things we do as a church and the way we do them matters. Programs and the curriculums that support them are not bad things; they are servants of something more

---

27 I have heard my good friend, Steve Hopkins, tell this story multiple times and with his permission, have paraphrased it for use here. Steve is the Group Leader for the Bible Teaching and Leadership Resource Group with the State Convention of Baptists in Ohio.

important. Ministry programs provide reproducible and sustainable strategies for empowering people to live on mission together. They are a means for developing followers of Christ who live into the fullness of life and mission as he intended. However, we are not defined by the programs or curriculums or ministry models we utilize. There is something deeper. And, when our context or culture calls for change, we had better be clear about what matters most.

Lesslie Newbigin—a groundbreaking missiologist of the last century—made this observation more than 35 years ago:

> The one thing that can certainly be said about this chapter of human history is that it is over. For more than two centuries it has provided the framework in which the Western churches have understood their task. Now we are forced to do something that the Western churches have never had to do since the days of their own birth—discover the form and substance of a missionary church...[28]

The Trauma of Success

Step into the whirlwind surrounding the day of Pentecost. Yesterday morning you were part of a faithful core of 120 who had known the sweet rhythms of that upper room experience. Your "church" was that comfortable size

---

28 Lesslie Newbigin: *The Open Secret: An Introduction to the Theology of Mission,* revised edition, 1995. Wm. B. Eerdmans. p.5.

where you knew everyone and everyone knew you. You shared the luxury of a tight relational dynamic.

Today that church you knew is gone.

As unforgettable as that unexpected outpouring of the Spirit was yesterday, the overwhelming growth of 3,000 new people[29] permanently wrecked your tight familiar fellowship. Yesterday your comfortably sized little band of believers exploded into a megachurch. The final count of exactly how many people said yes to Jesus yesterday is still uncertain, but it is clear that you will never fit into that upper room again.

So, what do you do now? What should life look like for a group this large? Where do you meet? When do you meet? What rhythms and practices matter most? How will you develop and deploy all of these new disciples into the fullness of life and mission Jesus intended?

Prior to this moment in human history, every follower of Jesus had been taught directly by Jesus himself. Now, suddenly, more than 3,000 brand new followers of Christ need to be formed as disciples without Jesus to do it. Jesus is no longer here in person, so, what will you do to help all of them learn to walk as Jesus walked?

What follows in Acts 2 describes the ways that first church learned to address these challenges. In the crucible of chaos created by this unmanageably huge number of new believers, the early church figured out how to live in a way that empowered followers of Jesus to live as his disciples.

---

29 The actual number of people might have been three-four times that many had the recorded count included men, women, and children. That could easily mean a church over 10,000. Even so, we are familiar with the number 3,000 and it is an adequate representation of the hyper-growth challenge they faced.

The community became the discipling environment. The rhythms of life they developed formed a community that empowers people to follow Jesus fully. This next juncture in their journey reveals the DNA of an apprenticing community.

Rhythms of an Apprenticing Community

With Jesus physically present, his followers literally walked with him from town to town. "Discipleship," as we call it, happened in the course of life directly at his side. They listened to him speak to crowds and they sat together during private teaching moments. They learned to pray as they saw his life of intimacy with the Father. They watched when miracles were performed, when demons were confronted, and when religious leaders tried to trap him in his words. They asked questions while they strolled the countryside. They were given ministry assignments when the crowds gathered and they were sent out to do ministry on their own. Jesus was the Rabbi and they were his disciples. To follow Jesus was to be apprenticed not only into relationship with him, but also into a life of mission that looked like his own.

Two thousand years later we are accustomed to the notion that Jesus is present through his Spirit although not in the flesh. The infant Church, in contrast, had to figure out how to carry on the work of Jesus for the first time. What Luke shows us is that the role of the Incarnate Rabbi is now a role shared by the community. In the same way that the Body of Christ embodies the mission of Jesus, the Body has been tasked to develop and deploy his followers. The Body of Christ is the apprenticing community—the community is the discipler.

We normally talk about the life of the church by discussing weekend services, familiar programs, special events on the calendar, and the like. Luke takes us down a different path. He interrupts our program-focused mindset by pointing us to the pattern of life they lived together. While we want a detailed plan to follow, he paints the picture with the quick stroke of a broad brush. The rhythms and priorities that shaped a transformational way of doing life together were what mattered. It is the description of life as an apprenticing community.

> They devoted themselves to the apostles' teaching and to the fellowship, to the breaking of bread and to prayer ... all the believers were together and had everything in common. Selling their possessions they gave to anyone as he had need. Every day they continued to meet together in the temple courts. They broke bread in their homes and ate together with glad and sincere hearts, praising God ...[30]

These are familiar words for most of us, perhaps so familiar that they have lost their punch. But, I invite you to consider that these descriptions mean much more than what most of us think of when we hear them. This short description portrays a non-compartmentalized view of church life where all of these factors were integrated into everything. These phrases do not describe five separate programs or stages of ministry life; they are an integrated whole that shape a life-

---

30 Acts 2.42-47

changing environment. In fact, this portrayal of the early church sounds very much like the experience of traveling at the side of Jesus as one of his disciples.

We talk a lot about the need for community these days. Here, Luke gives us a holistic view what that community looks like. It is a simple approach that invites us to imagine what church life might look like if we could start over.

Essential Rhythms

Start with the end in mind. They needed to create an environment that would disciple this ever-increasing flow of new believers into the fullness of what it means to follow Jesus. They needed a way to develop new followers into witnesses. What emerged may not satisfy our human desire for something we can "plug and play," but it invites us into a rhythm of life that will transform everything we do. Luke describes five dynamic priorities that provide the heart of a game plan without scripting the plays.

No matter what your ministry model is, no matter what your core programs are, these five components of life together build a transformational environment. The community becomes an apprenticing environment when life together is lived this way.

ONE: *DEVOTION TO THE APOSTLES' TEACHING*

The apostles were the living repositories of all Jesus had said and done. By attending to the teaching of the apostles, this young body of believers gave constant focus on the life and teaching and heart of Jesus. This devotion means their life together was shaped by a desire to know Jesus, to discover intimacy with him, to be apprenticed into the values of the kingdom, and to align themselves with his mission in the world. It implies relentless attention to everything the apostles had learned in the presence of Jesus.

This devotion meant so much more than our current focus on teaching as the acquisition of biblical content. In the Western world today, we believe teaching has happened when the teacher has covered his or her material. In the ancient world—and most of the non-Western world today— teaching has not happened until the student has acted on what they were taught.[31] Devotion to the apostles' teaching in this context has as much to do with obedience as it does to understanding.

An uncomfortable reality is that contemporary evangelicalism has discipled people into lives of disobedience. No, we don't teach that obedience is unimportant, but obedience to everything we are taught is not expected. As consummate consumers, we are well trained in the art of picking and choosing what we like. Sunday mornings or small group Bible studies are no different. We leave with good ideas but without a commitment to action. Devotion to the apostles' teaching meant the community worked together to help one another put that teaching into practice. They were devoted not just to the content of the teaching, but to living by it as well. They were attentive to application not merely the acquisition of more biblical information.

---

31   I am grateful to David Broodryk for articulating this distinction during a workshop he led in London on Making Movements in November 2012.

TWO: *Devotion to the Fellowship*

Unfortunately, these days the word fellowship drips with over-worn religiosity. "Koinonia" is not the Greek word for that green bean, crunchy onion, and mushroom soup casserole served at every church potluck. Fellowship is not a label for coffee and donuts served in the courtyard or an event that happens some evening for church people.

On the contrary, the word for fellowship might better be translated as partnership, the practice of *mutual interdependence*. The partnership implied by "koinonia" implies a transformational environment where people share their lives and participate in one another's growth. Life on life is where accountability, encouragement, and personal growth takes place. This kind of partnership is where we "stimulate one another to love and good deeds."[32] No wonder this kind of devotion led to people contributing to meet the needs of others. Fellowship like this means authentic and sacrificial community where everyone is both recipient and contributor. It infers a level of engagement together that cannot be accomplished when we only meet for one or two structured hours a week.

There is an African proverb that says, "If you want to go fast, go alone. If you want to go far, go together."

We were made to go far, *together*.

---

32 Hebrews 10.24

THREE: *DEVOTION TO THE BREAKING OF BREAD*

Yes, "the breaking of bread" became a pseudonym for the Lord's Supper, but at the core it meant they ate together. In fact, just in case we failed to get it the first time, Luke repeats himself in verse 46.

Think about how many times the Gospel narratives tell us Jesus shared a meal with people. It is a simple principle. Eating together is part of doing life together. Something deep and rich and life-giving takes place when people share a meal. Very few moments in life are as pregnant with potential as the unguarded informal conversations that take place over food. It means that conversations about the apostles' teaching, times of prayer, worship, and ministry to others happened in both formal and informal settings.

Somewhere along the way, we adopted a pattern where "ministry" and discipleship were separated from everyday life and informal settings. We believe that we participate in the formation of people through structured appointments and curriculums. In so doing, we bisect life into categories of spiritual and secular. We act as if spiritually significant moments are formal and planned. But, Luke is telling us that a great deal of the transformational power of the early church grew out of their constant pattern of integrating the apostles' teaching, prayer, and the Lord's Supper into the exchanges of everyday life—unguarded personal interaction over meals in particular.

FOUR: *DEVOTION TO PRAYER*

Nothing of lasting kingdom significance can be accomplished in our own strength. So, it is no surprise that this explosive season in the life of the church was permeated by prayer. We will look closer at the role of prayer as a key to the spiritual power of the early church in a later chapter, but for now we cannot gloss over the fact that one of five dimensions of life for this fledgling church was a devotion to prayer. Without playing the guilt card too strongly, it takes very little imagination to consider the revolutionary potential of a church where prayer captured 20 percent of its attention.

FIVE: *GENEROSITY FOR ANYONE IN NEED*

When God is at work in his people, there is a consistent pattern of engagement with the poor and the marginalized. His heart for the poor shows up throughout the Scriptures and his judgment for ignoring the poor stands out just as clearly. So, it should come as no surprise that here in the earliest days of life in the church, God's heart for the poor takes on new levels of practical expression. This is no token project or simple all-church offering conducted annually. They demonstrated the ongoing pattern of sacrificial response to meet the needs of others.

Luke's description here seems to imply that the needs being met at this point in time were those needs among the emerging body of believers. I would simply argue that by normalizing a pattern of meeting the needs of those who couldn't meet their own, the early church demonstrated a heart of responsiveness to the poor. It is a kingdom value in action. It is also one of the ways that the church of the current day can demonstrate the redemptive power of the Good News to a world that has stopped listening. The way we care for our own and the way we care for the marginalized sends a louder message than the words we use.

Gathering Places

We struggle to conceive of church life without thinking of a building and formally planned services. Yet, they had neither. Facing the immediate challenge of discipling 3,000 new Christians into the fullness of following Jesus, they had to solve the problem of gathering places. Their solution? Use everything. They met in the expansive courtyards of the Temple, they met in homes, and although Luke doesn't say so, I would guess they met on hillsides and under trees as well. They simply used every normal gathering place available as a venue for these rhythms of life. Revolutionary.

Their focus was not on the place where they met, but on the pattern of life that defined the way they met together. Forming disciples came first and a church resulted. You see, if we require a building to be a church, then we are actually not being the church.

In light of the growth of house church movements in recent decades, I need to add a few comments about what Luke is *not* saying here. This passage does not make a case for house churches as *the preferred* model for doing church better. House churches are clearly one ministry model, but, in this passage, Luke tells us that this church met in public and in private, formally and informally, in large groups and in small ones. They continued to meet in Temple Courts *and* they met from house to house. It was not an either/or, but a both/and. The church was the people and the way they did life together was their discipleship strategy. It has never been about the place.

More Freedom – Less Judgment

Thinking about the DNA of our daily life this way invites a great deal of creativity and cuts away a great deal of ecclesiastical clutter. It is very possible that much of what we do is less necessary than we think it is. If we had the courage to go back to the drawing board and look for ways to normalize these five dimensions of life into a fewer number of core programs, what might it look like? What if we could trim down some of the extensive menu of our programs? By putting a little more breathing room into the church calendar, we might breathe a little more oxygen into pastors and ministry leaders exhausted by their role as ringleaders of a 24-7 church program. By doing less we could deploy more people to do more in response to the needs of a lost world.

Over recent decades, a large number of fresh approaches have been tried as ways to engage a changing culture and more effectively make disciples. In the late 1970's the seeker-sensitive model was launched. The house-church and simple-church models then offered a way to scale back from high-production and complex programming approaches. Recently, we have watched megachurches morph into multi-site congregations. Simultaneously, ministry models are developing around neo-monastic, cell-based, liturgical, hyper-informal, video-venue, cowboy culture, and who knows how many other approaches.

Is there a best model? Are there models of ministry that we should be concerned about? The essence of our DNA as a community speaks to the kind of environment that will apprentice followers of Jesus into the life he intended. The question we face is not which ministry models are good or bad, but, how do we live so that becoming and multiplying disciples of Jesus is *the focus* of our life together?

Luke shows us the rhythms of life that will form an apprenticing community. What he leaves us with is the freedom to integrate those rhythms in our own way as culture and context change. As a matter of fact, if you start tracing the journey of the church through the changes within the book of Acts, you find they had to change the way they did life as a church repeatedly. The first expression of the early church was as a tight-knit group of 120 meeting regularly in an upper room. After the day of Pentecost they were a megachurch and had to start over. The pattern of life described in Acts 2 only lasted for a few chapters. When persecution came in Acts 7-8, it blew up everything. Within a few short chapters in the book of Acts, we find the church starting over and finding new ways to do what mattered most. It is a pattern that gives us freedom to do the same.

21st Century Drawing Board

So, how does this help us? How do the lessons of this infant church speak to an era where there is so much diversity in the shape and style of local churches? Does the DNA of their approach offer hope or help to the many congregations that are struggling these days? Let me suggest three take away insights.

1. Focus

Focus on developing and deploying disciples.

The clarity of Acts 2 gets us out of the muddle that comes from trying to manage programs, staff, congregational tensions, building needs, financial pressures, and everything else that competes for leadership attention. It calls us into a focused conversation about whether the way we are doing life together develops followers of Christ into disciples who will reproduce themselves.

Organizational life has uncanny gravity. It pulls us into thinking about the church as if building and sustaining the institution were what mattered most. Programmatic gravity draws our attention to the maintenance of different ministry programs as if their survival measures our success. Focusing on making disciples who are making disciples is the way to counteract that gravity.

A paradox of church life is that when we focus on building a church we get an organization, even an institution. When we focus on making and developing disciples we end up with a dynamic church.

2. LIBERTY

We have tremendous liberty in the way we live out the rhythms of community life Luke described. There are no restrictive prescriptions and there are no secret formulas.

The transformational power of the Body of Christ is released when these rhythms become the substance of life in community. They are not a series of prescriptive steps. We have freedom to experiment, to be creative, and to explore different ways of living as a community of believers. We have freedom to be nimble and responsive to a culture in flux. Just as the early church had the freedom to figure out new ways of doing life after the upper room no longer worked, we have freedom to experiment with ways to integrate these rhythms into every part of life together.

Apply this thinking specifically to the way we think about discipleship. Poll a group of established Christians about what discipleship means and I am fairly certain you will hear descriptions of a highly structured, content-oriented, intensive weekly approach led by some Gandalf-like master. It is a strategy that is hard to normalize across the entire church. There aren't many Gandalfs. When you understand that the community is the discipler, you open the gates for everyone to participate. Our endgame is about multiplying and developing disciples who will follow Jesus and will help others do the same. How we build apprenticing communities where that happens is an opportunity for amazing freedom.

3. ENVIRONMENT

It is time to pay more attention to the environments we create than the curriculum we employ.

We have become experts at creating and following curriculums and study guides. These tools are helpful, but of their own accord, they do not create the environment Luke described in Acts 2. Furthermore, most of our curriculums emphasize the exploration and acquisition of information. Think of it like a complex recipe. You can have all the ingredients you need (content) but the way you assemble them and the way you cook them (environment) determines everything.

The rhythms of life we find in Acts 2 describe the environment of life in the early church. It is an environment where followers of Christ were transformed. They committed themselves to one another, they lived lives of prayer, they devoted themselves to understanding and obeying the apostles' teaching, they shared life and meals and worship together, and they met real needs. The way they did life—the environment they created—taught them to follow Jesus in all of his fullness.

When we get to chapter eight in the book of Acts, Luke will show us exactly how effective this environment was for developing the kind of disciples we long to see produced by our efforts. Here in response to the overwhelming influx of new believers, Luke shows us the rhythms of a transformational community. This way of life is in our DNA. We were made for it. And, when we live accordingly, a revolutionary community of disciples is unleashed on the world. The question for all of us is, what are the rhythms of life we are cultivating in the community of faith we call home?

five

More than an Organism

LIVE that odd pattern of contemporary life where flying on a plane a few times a month is a normal activity. While most of my friends find it dizzying, I simply think of it as commuting to work. I am long past any sense of glamour or stress about flying. That little seat in a noisy tube provides a unique place to step off the grid. Most of the time when I get on a plane I want it to be a place of escape, quiet, retreat.

Translated, that means I usually don't want to talk to the person next to me. I don't want to see pictures of their kids or hear about their job and, although there have been a few dramatic exceptions, I don't plan to witness to the person next to me. OK, call me a bad person.

Over the years, I have learned a few tricks about how to dissuade the eager conversationalist. If I *don't* want to talk, I respond to the obligatory "What do you do?" by telling them I used to be a pastor and now I do training, mentoring, and consulting with pastors and churches. That answer seems to stir fear that I might be primed to unload the evangelistic dump truck. Most of the time, they reply with a puzzled "hrumpf" before leaning back and immersing themselves in a book.

On the other hand, if I do want to talk, I find that I need to be a bit clever so that my response doesn't shut the conversation down. If it were not for a little thing called airplane security, the answer I would love to give is, "I train leaders to create revolutionary movements." I still might use that line one of these days.

Not long ago I was on a flight preparing for a presentation on the life cycle of a local church. At one point the passenger next to me leaned over and apologized for interrupting me. He had been eavesdropping on my PowerPoint™ slides and was desperate to know more about what I was working on. I walked him through the heart of the presentation and we started talking. The more we talked the more he told me about the struggles of his church. He loves his pastor and highly respects him, but the church is a mess as an organization. The ways they do business, run committees, make decisions—the organizational structures and systems—are sucking the life out of the church and out of the pastor. He asked for a copy of my notes and permission to share our conversation with his pastor.

I can only make guesses about the real issues facing my fellow passenger's church, but I work with congregations of all types and know firsthand that organizational structures in most churches need help. In fact, as often as not, organizational structures in the church are hindering the church's mission and draining the life of its leaders. Rather than increasing our capacity for ministry impact they consume our human capital. Rather than empowering workers and leaders with the authority and resources they need to initiate kingdom-focused ministry, unhealthy structures frustrate and constrain people. Rather than developing revolutionaries, we nurture bureaucrats.

The capacity for growth and sustainable impact for any movement relates directly to its effectiveness at developing appropriate organizational structures. The church is no exception. We speak often of the church as an organism. However, many fail to grasp that organization and organism complement rather than compete with one another. The early church discovered the role of healthy structures when an organizational meltdown nearly derailed everything.

A Multi-Layered Crisis

Acts 6 opens with the description of a three dimensional crisis.

> In those days, when the number of disciples was increasing, the Grecian Jews among them complained against the Hebraic Jews because their widows were being overlooked in the daily distribution of food.[33]

---

33 Acts 6.1

1ST THE VISIBLE PROBLEM:
GREEK WIDOWS WERE GOING HUNGRY!

Greek widows in Israel were women with no recourse. With no husband, no rights in Israel, and no means of support, these women were literally at the mercy of others. If they were being bypassed in the distribution of food, they were at risk of starvation. Some have speculated that among the large groups of God-fearers who made a pilgrimage to Israel for the Passover holidays, there may have been many widows who became followers of Christ and remained as part of the newly formed church. Now, they not only faced the troubles of widowhood, but being unwanted Christians exacerbated their vulnerabilities. They needed help. Without assistance they might literally starve to death.

2ND THE DEEPER PROBLEM:
ACCUSATION OF INSTITUTIONALIZED RACISM!

The Greek widows need food and their real problem is of foremost importance, but look closer. Grecian Jews were complaining of systemic mistreatment by Hebraic Jews. These Greek widows were being overlooked by the system through which the daily distribution of food took place. This represents more than an attitude problem and more than a mistake. The real accusation is that of systematized discrimination against the Greek widows—institutionalized racism.

3ʳᵈ THE SILENT PROBLEM:
DAMAGE TO THE TESTIMONY OF THE GOSPEL!

If the Gospel is good news for all men everywhere, how could the bearers of this Good News actively discriminate against another segment of mankind? If God is the father to the fatherless, a husband to the widow, and tenderhearted toward the poor, then how could his people propagate treatment like this? How could a people who claim to embody the Good News create a practice of such bad news? What would those who observed this behavior believe about the Savior these people claimed to follow?

You see, when our organizational systems and structures break down, there are waves of impact that touch people in ways we are not aware of. People surrounding us listen to the apologetics of our behavior as much or even more than the rhetoric of our lips.

I know that for many of us, so much of the Scriptures are so familiar that we read through accounts like this at hundreds of words per minute. But we must slow down to consider all that was at stake. The crisis recorded in Acts 6 was a massive wake-up call. The organizational systems were broken and there were huge consequences.

This situation demonstrates a helpful principle for leaders as they monitor the organizations they lead. When you have good people with good intentions attempt to do good work and in the process keep hurting one another, you have broken systems.

In our current day, there is an interesting dichotomy. On the one hand, some people feel that organizational structures and systems are inherently suspect. Ministry should be organic, relational. It should flow naturally without being tied up by the limitations of organizational structure. (A wave of recent church planting started with this philosophy only to discover that after a few years and early growth, the young church exhausts its leaders and cannot maintain sustainability.)

On the other hand, some folks feel the tides of change tugging at their traditions and are trying to lock down favorite organizational structures and methods. In this camp, the way we do things is not to be touched. To both groups, I want to argue that anytime the mission of the church is hindered by what we are doing, not doing, or by the way we are doing it, we must find a better way and make whatever changes are needed.

Luke peels back the curtain of this highly combustible moment because in it we see the early church go back to the drawing board. It was a highly vulnerable moment where the desperate need for a solution caused them to re-tool again. They had to learn how to manage the organizational needs of a growing movement without squelching its revolutionary nature.

Courageous Leadership

I think I admire courage in leadership more than any other single trait. Watching the apostles step up to address this crisis inspires me. They were not defensive, did not cast blame, did not spiritualize the problem away, and did not hide behind a façade of prayer as a stall tactic. They faced the problem head on and took action.

When the apostles stepped up to propose a solution to the congregation, they announced a radical shift in the way things were going to work. They proposed sweeping change to the church's leadership structure. Until this point in time, the infant church operated with the same leadership structure Jesus put in place—a team of twelve. By identifying new roles for leaders, differentiating responsibilities between leaders, and appointing seven new people to fill these roles, they were putting aside the structure Jesus had given them and implementing something never tried before.

In contemporary language, they moved from working relationally as an informally managed team to a whole new level of organizational structure. They expanded the pastoral staff from 12 to 19, created an Organizational Chart, introduced job descriptions, and narrowed the role of the apostles. (FYI: When you look at the role of the seven in the chapters that follow, it is clear these were not food service staff. In church practice of the current day, these were pastoral staff positions.)

> It would not be right for us to neglect the ministry of the word of God in order to wait on tables. Brothers, choose seven men from among you who are known to be full of the Spirit and wisdom. We will turn this responsibility over to them and will give our attention to prayer and the ministry of the word.[34]

---

34 Acts 6.2-4

Let's not kid ourselves. This was a bold move. Most of us have been in the room or at least heard about times when churches blew up over much smaller decisions. These guys were not promoting some recent ecclesiological trend, they were tampering with the structure of leadership Jesus himself established. They courageously acknowledged that the initial leadership structure no longer served the body or the mission well. They were desperate to find a better way.

Although the leadership team of twelve worked well when there were 120 gathered in the upper room, the size of the congregation is now staggering. Acts 4 tells us that the number of *men* in the church was 5,000.[35] Add to that number women, children, and all the additional people who became followers of Christ between Acts 4 and Acts 6 and a conservative guesstimate would put this church at more than 20,000 people by this time. No wonder things were breaking down. I have heard that Peter Drucker recommended you completely restructure your organization anytime it grows by more than 50 precent.[36] Growth from 120 to 20,000 is an increase of 16,700 percent!

Effective systems and structures align behavior, priorities, money, programs, and people around mission. They empower leaders to act by clarifying responsibility and authority and by providing adequate resourcing. They divide the workload of ministry by effectively distributing it throughout the body. They facilitate communication and decision making. They nurture new leaders and initiatives in ways that stimulate creative energy throughout the body.

---

35   Acts 4.4

36   Source unknown.

In short, effective organizational systems and structures have both a supportive and a catalytic function. In the church, healthy organization increases our capacity for the transforming work of developing and deploying disciples.

To look at it another way, healthy organizational structures work like the fence surrounding an elementary school playground. The absence of a fence creates insecurity that causes kids to stay huddled near the middle of the playground. Put up a fence and those same kids will run and play and hoot and holler from edge to edge of the entire expanse. When we get it right, instead of constraining people, healthy organizational structures infuse energy and freedom into the people of our ministries. We literally give people room to run and play with joy.

Following the mind-boggling growth of those early days, this young church ran into a wall. Rather than releasing people and new energy for ministry, their breakdown put a strangle hold on the life of the community. It was dividing people, creating suspicion between factions, and quickly distracting everyone from the main thing. The solution called for addressing the complicated root problem. The only hitch? Announcing changes on a scale like this can get sticky.

A Congregational Meeting

Chalk it up to my sick sense of humor or to the fact that I have been in way too many congregational business meetings, but I cannot help thinking that if a change like this had been proposed in some of the churches I know, it would bring out more than a few cantankerous responses.

So, let's have a little fun. Imagine you are a fly on the wall in that congregational meeting when these plans went public.

During the first part of the meeting, the apostles review the problem and then present a solution—their plan to restructure the leadership of the church. When they are done, they open it up to discussion. Immediately the questions and resistance begin.

The first hand goes up. "Hold everything. Jesus appointed the 12 as apostles of the church. What right do we have to add others?"

Then another, "God's number has always been 12! 12 sons of Jacob; 12 tribes of Israel; 12 spies; 12 books of history in the Old Testament; and 12 minor prophets."

Interrupting, "That's right. Jesus chose *12* apostles? So, where do we get off adding a group of 7?"

"I disagree. The problem is not with adding 7 more. Seven is God's number, it is the perfect number. But adding 7 gives us 19 leaders. Who can explain the rationale for having 19 leaders? You can't find the number 19 anywhere in the scriptures."

Another theme of debate begins. "What's the big deal about the number? Who cares if we have 12 or 7 or 19, the fatal flaw in this plan is all this talk of job descriptions. Organizational charts and job descriptions are methods straight out of the business world. Why do we need to capitulate to the culture and start incorporating business strategies in God's church?"

The heat in the room grows as the conversation fractures.

After a few moments of chaos, another dominant voice grabs everyone's attention. "None of you get it. The real problem we have is that the church has grown too big. Becoming a megachurch is evidence that we have compromised the Gospel. The only way to explain the fact that we are attracting so many people is that we have become too worldly. We must not be preaching the full cost of following Jesus."

"We are growing too fast," says another. "Shouldn't we cut back on evangelism and take care of ourselves first? This problem with food for these widows shows we are not caring for all the people we already have. We don't even know everyone anymore!"

The rumbling mutters onward. Finally, a normally quiet man in the back corner gets the attention of the crowd and asks his question. "I just want to know one thing. With these new leaders and this new division of responsibilities, does this mean that if I am in the hospital, the apostles won't come visit me anymore?"

Granted, my fictitious congregational meeting cannot be found in Acts 6. I use it to make the point that this proposal meant real change and called for real courage. The uncertainty of change is troubling for most people and makes us look for some piece of certainty to hang onto. But, they had no finger of God writing on tablets of stone, outlining a plan for a retooled leadership structure. It was a plan that just made sense. And, they had the courage to go forward with it. They were willing to experiment with new leadership dynamics, personnel, and structured responsibilities. It was a savvy move to appoint bi-cultural leaders, but it was still an experiment in finding a new way forward. Luke summarizes, "the proposal pleased the group."[37] They embraced the important role of organizational structures and made changes intended to increase their potential for impact as a movement.

The Death Spiral of Organizational Breakdown

One of the best ways to derail the impact of a church is to embroil her leaders in conflict and overwork so that they are unable to focus on the strategic issues. The Twelve were at risk, even though the presenting issue was the widows. You sense the toll of this organizational breakdown on the Twelve in their comments. "It would not be right for us to neglect the ministry of the word of God in order to wait on tables."[38] Said in a different way, "we have grown so much and so fast, that we feel the tension of trying to meet all the needs. We need to focus on the part of the work that only we can do and to make that happen we need help." Without additional manpower, this was a setup for burnout. It is the classic recipe for keeping the attention of your leaders focused on the wrong things. The Twelve were in as much need as the Greek widows.

Leaders pay a price for flawed organizational structures today as well. From my work with pastors and church boards, I have concluded that the majority of churches have just about perfected an organizational structure designed for a church two stages of growth behind where they are right

---

37   Acts 6.5

38   Acts 6.2

now. Regardless of whether the size of the congregation is increasing or decreasing, we hold onto old structures and old ways of operating far beyond the time when they served us well.

Not long ago a pastor from a church of less than 100 told me his constitution mandated more than *60 different positions* on church boards and committees. That is crazy. Unwieldy organizational structures suck the life out of leaders. I guarantee, broken systems will pull leaders away from a life of witness and into the quagmire of institutional maintenance. When leaders live in that space, everyone and everything suffers. Any sense of compelling kingdom purpose evaporates.

When things aren't working well, the "Avis syndrome" takes over—everyone tries working harder. Where there was once a willingness to take bold risks for the kingdom, in its place arises a drive to preserve and protect. The fear of "getting it wrong" looms larger than the potential of getting it right.

Splintered community, discouraged and distracted leaders, risk-averse congregations, mission erosion, and witness evaporation are all part of the death spiral launched by broken systems and structures. It may not be quick, but it is ugly.

Factors like these amplify the significance of what the early church did that day. In their response to this crisis, they made a declaration to all of us. Yes, we are a revolutionary movement, but the way we organize ourselves matters. The DNA of the church is built around our mission, not around our structures. The organizational structures and systems we create are temporary means to support the transformational nature of our witness. They are not sacred. They are not to be preserved at all cost. They are servants of our assignment to declare and demonstrate the Good News of Jesus. When they get in the way, change them. Have the courage to try what makes the most sense. Don't wait for a solution that seems perfect.

Rejuvenated Impact

Yes, I know, talking about organizational systems and structures has about as much sex appeal as a turnip. That is, until you connect these organizational matters with the revolutionary results that followed.

Luke tells us that after making the changes proposed that day, the impact of the early church exploded again. The changes they made were not some pedantic attempt to simply make things work better. Underneath it all, this organizational re-structuring was all about their capacity for mission—their ability to live as the incarnate presence of Jesus. And, their experiment succeeded wildly! Luke names three waves of expansion that resulted.[39]

1. "The Word of God spread!"

They had a viral explosion of the Gospel. They had none of the print or media tools of our modern day, but they did have an unstoppable movement fueled by firsthand reports of people who would not stop talking.

---

39 Acts 6.7

2. "The number of disciples increased rapidly."

I love this phrase! Rapid increase sounds a bit like the day of Pentecost all over again. Revolutionary capacity for expansion was released when the organizational stuff got cleaned up. I wonder what might be released if we took a courageous look at our structures as well. It seems that sometimes we are satisfied with slow, incremental response to the good news of the Gospel. Is it possible that our structures create a chokehold on our capacity for explosive impact?

3. "A large number of priests became obedient to the faith."

Priests and other religious leaders were the opposition. They were the most hostile, unresponsive, hardest people to reach. These religious leaders represent the kind of people who are easy to give up on as a lost cause. No one expects these people to respond to the Gospel. But, notice, not only did they respond, they came to Christ in *large numbers!*

Thinking Differently

Packed into the dynamics of this moment in Acts 6 are lessons and insights that interrupt our organizational belief systems and address ways we get stuck as the church in the twenty-first century.

END OF THE ORGANISM VS. ORGANIZATION DEBATE

Enough already. The debate over the church as organism versus organization is decidedly misguided and leads to strawman arguments. Unchecked, this love-hate approach sabotages our ability to talk about the strategic role of organizational systems to empower the organic work of ministry. Simply put, it has never been an either/or issue. Both matter. In fact, our mission demands that we pay as much attention to our support systems as we do to our message. Healthy organizational structures serve the revolutionary impact of our mission.

Institutionalism, on the other hand, is an entirely different concern. While organizational structures and systems exist to empower ministry, institutionalism takes over when building or maintaining structures becomes the end instead of the means. Institutions are about stability, preservation, heritage, and predictability. Revolutionary movements are about changing the world and understand everything else exists to serve that mission.

STRUCTURES ARE NEITHER PERFECT NOR PERMANENT

Whenever church size, local context, or culture changes, the way we organize ourselves to carry out ministry needs to adapt as well. As a matter of fact, consider this. We don't find leadership described in the same language at any other time in the New Testament. Before long, we see the emergence of elders. Later as the church continued to expand deeper into the Roman Empire we find they adapted regional oversight structures that paralleled the Roman civil government.[40]

---

40 See, "The two structures of God's redemptive mission," by Ralph Winter. This seminal article has been published and republished in multiple circles and can easily be found online.

The point is that even within the early decades of the church, different leadership approaches and structures were developed.

WHEN LEADERS ARE IN CONFLICT, LOOK DEEPER

Relational tensions between leaders are generally easy to spot. But, this episode reminds us that when conflict develops, there might very well be an organizational breakdown lying beneath the surface. Remember, when you have good people trying to do good work with good motives and they hurt each other in the process, you have a systems problem.

DE-SPIRITUALIZE THE CONVERSATION

Because the structures of our ministry are so closely connected to the mission of our ministry, it is easy to speak of them in spiritualized tones and words. However, the more we spiritualize our organizational structures, the more difficult it is to honestly evaluate what is working and what is not. As soon as someone says anything that sounds like, "this is the way they did things in the early church," it is almost impossible to have non-emotionally charged conversation. If the early church had the freedom to tamper with the leadership structure Jesus himself instituted, we are on good ground to evaluate and experiment with organizational approaches that might work better in our context. It is OK to treat the church constitution as a working document—a helpful tool—that never was on par with the Scriptures.

A Place to Start

In order to pull this conversation out of the realm of the theoretical and into the zone of personal significance, let's perform what I call the Acts 2 Test. Imagine that when you arrive at your worship service this weekend, your church has instantly jumped to quadruple its current size. Suddenly and permanently, four times as many people are part of your congregation.

What are all the things about the way your church is structured that will not work well anymore? Where will current structures get in the way? How will decision making processes need to be altered? How will you communicate with everyone in the congregation? What are you not doing now that you will need to start doing? How will you apprentice all of these people into the life Jesus intended? How will leaders be developed and empowered with authority to lead this many people? How will large numbers of people be mobilized to share the workload of ministry—not just within church, but as witnesses on mission to your community?

I find that no one really knows what would be needed if their church instantly quadrupled in size. The very exercise of trying imagine that scenario causes people to recognize organizational issues that need to be addressed right now. Those issues that surface for you when you ask these questions are probably barriers already hindering the transformational potential of your church today.

As the Holy Spirit shaped the DNA of the early church, he shaped *us* to be a people who subordinate organizational matters to our mission. But, that does not mean he wants us to ignore organizational issues. He gave us freedom and flexibility. He asks us to trust him enough to resist entrenchment and the gravity of institutionalism. He imbued us with the courage to address, change, and even experiment with systems and structures that will extend our capacity for impact.

six

Explosive Multiplication

F you attended Sunday School or Vacation Bible School as a kid, there are certain little rhymes and routines you can still say by memory. Here's one:

> This is the church
> and this is the steeple
> open the doors
> and there's all the people.

It was a cute little ditty whose hand motions made Sunday School a bit more interactive. I know it was intended to make the experience of learning fun and cultivate a love for the church. Yet, it also anchored distinctive ecclesiology into our minds and our kinesthetic memories. The problem is, it was horrible theology.

Think about it. That little ritual taught us that the church is a building or, at the very least, requires one. We learned that a real church building conforms to certain iconic norms. (Warehouses would be highly suspect.) Once you build or acquire the right kind of building, your goal is to fill it. If you are a pastor or church leader, the number of people you gather and keep in your building defines the measure of your success. If you are a church member, what it means to be a "successful" Christian is to be inside the building whenever the doors are open.

Now, extend that thinking to the realm of church planting. Any notion of planting a new church triggers an avalanche of pre-conceived thoughts about the challenges of real estate, buildings, finances, and the need to gather a crowd of Christians who will fill the pews. In our minds starting a new church implies the whole enchilada from the steeple to the pew. It is nearly impossible to conceive of church planting without simultaneously thinking of the entire package.

If the challenges of buildings, programs, and money weren't enough to dissuade most of us from entertaining the possibility of church planting, our typical parish mindset will. We tend to view our city as "our territory" and other churches as our competitors. Church plants feel like a threat because we expect them to compete with us for members from the pool of people who are already Christians. The problem is, we are focused on the small slice of the population pre-disposed to embracing the church rather than viewing our city as a mission field filled with people who need to discover Jesus.

In Acts 8, Luke will turn a great deal of our thinking upside down as he invites us to see the multiplication of new churches as the normal life of the church.

You see, healthy things give birth to new life. Whether plants, animals, or people, healthy things reproduce. The same principle applies to the Christian life. Healthy Christians reproduce themselves by making disciples and healthy churches reproduce themselves through new churches. [41] The reproductive process is both evidence of and a pathway to health.

An Accidental Movement

Jesus was clear in his mandate in Acts 1.8 and Matthew 28. His mission goes far beyond establishing the church in the land of Israel. He envisioned a movement that would extend to the ends of the earth and he commissioned all of us as instruments of that movement. However, at the conclusion of Acts 7, the early church was still anchored in Jerusalem. It was a situation about to change forever.

Stephen's martyrdom telegraphed the launch of full-scale persecution and the end of church life as they knew it. The days when Jewish leaders were satisfied to harass a few representatives of this Christian movement screeched to a halt as widespread life-threatening attack was unleashed upon the church in Jerusalem. Chapter 8 of Acts begins with one sentence that says it all. "On that day a great persecution broke out."

---

41   Christian Schwartz, *Natural Church Development*. ChurchSmart Resources, 1996.

A great persecution indeed. What we skim over in a few words represents personal tragedy and trauma for those early followers of Christ. We know what this meant. Thanks to modern media we have all been exposed to stories of atrocity and abuse inflicted on the helpless by those in power. Persecution means people suffered and enough people suffered badly enough for everyone to fear for their lives. The language of Luke's summary, the dispersion of the church that followed, the example made with Stephen, and what we know from Paul's own personal testimony tells us this was brutal. Men and women were beaten, injured, and killed.

> Saul began to destroy the church. Going from house to house he dragged off men and women and put them in prison.[42]

Our brothers and sisters in those early days had few options. They could flee or go to prison or worse. Religious zealots with a vigilante thirst for blood were hunting them down. So they did what they had to do to protect their lives and their families.

Everyone fled.

> "On that day a great persecution broke out against the church at Jerusalem and all except the apostles were scattered throughout Judea and Samaria."[43]

---

42 Acts 8.3

43 Acts 8.1 (emphasis added)

The first church lost its entire congregation! This amazing community—those people who shared everything—saw the sweet season of those early days destroyed. No longer could they meet in the beautiful courtyard of the temple. No longer could they meet in one another's homes. Familiar rhythms of life and the life-giving gatherings of this church were finished. Relationships were torn apart. They had to start over.

The unexpected twist in the story is that Saul's plan backfired. Just when we modern-day readers begin to appreciate the substance of their sorrow, Luke reveals something none of us would have expected. Saul set out to extinguish the church, but instead, this persecution unleashed a church planting explosion. Instead of destroying the church, he succeeded in deploying the members of this congregation throughout all of Israel and Samaria and beyond. They did not scatter and hide. Members of that first congregation became missionaries.

> Those who had been scattered preached the word wherever they went.[44]

Look closely. Everyone except for the apostles scattered and every scattered person began preaching the word everywhere they went. *Everyone.* Not just a select or gifted few. They lived the life of witnesses wherever they went. It was not a managed strategy, it was simply what came naturally. It was the norm for every Christ-follower. If you have any question about the success of the rhythms of discipleship started in Acts 2, what happened when people were scattered

---

44 Acts 8.4

demonstrates stunning success. Luke could have written, "as these believers scattered they did what every follower of Christ normally did. They introduced new people to Jesus and gathered those new followers into communities of life and mission—new churches—wherever they went." This was an everyman movement.

Surprising? These believers lacked the decades of teaching and nurturing common to so many members of our contemporary churches. Yet, they succeeded in doing what most Christians in the pew today feel inadequate to do. They lived the mandate of Acts 1 as if doing anything otherwise never occurred to them. That's the thing about DNA: unless something gets in the way, it just works.

It is About Joy...Not Duty

What if our DNA as followers of Christ and as the Body of Christ was biased toward multiplication? What if the new normal for every church was to multiply new churches at great frequency? Experience has shown us that church planting continues to be one of the most effective ways to reach new people and new groups of people for Christ.

Luke walks us deeper into the story of what happened by using an effective literary approach. Rather than talking in broad generalities about everyone everywhere, Luke unpacks the details of one representative story. The account of Philip in an unnamed town of Samaria represents the pattern of the whole movement. By focusing on one person, the implication is that similar stories could be told about everywhere people went.

> Philip went down to a city in Samaria and proclaimed the Christ there. When the crowds heard Philip and saw the miraculous signs he did, they all paid close attention to what he said. With shrieks, evil spirits came out of many and many paralytics and cripples were healed. So there was great joy in that city.[45]

Did you catch that last phrase? The result of his presence and ministry was *great joy for that city*!

Living as a witness, engaging with people in a way that brings healing to the brokenness and evil in our world, and establishing new churches in order to multiply those efforts is so much more than a matter of duty. It is the pathway to joy. Theirs and ours!

It is time to deconstruct our notions of witness as obligation and discover that participation in the mission of Jesus is the path to joy. This way of life breathes joy into a local church, and just as significantly, into the community surrounding us. Imagine the impact on the region as what took place in this Samaritan town was repeated in town after town. This movement of multiplication meant people, communities, cities, even regions were transformed by the redemptive work of Jesus through his people. New disciples were made, those disciples formed themselves into new churches, the movement exploded, and joy was released.[46]

In contrast to this kind of joy, it seems that despair grips our cities today. City budgets are in crisis. Schools struggle

---

45 Acts 8.5-8

46 The church in Antioch, introduced in Acts 11.19, is an example of the direct results of this persecution.

under the weight of vanishing resources and expanding class sizes. Single parents fight for survival. Racial and immigration issues polarize our neighborhoods. Gangs and crime plague our urban centers. I could go on and on. Just as God used Philip to cast out evil and bring healing to those who were crippled, what if we could multiply local churches that would live out their witness with a healing presence in a broken world? What if every local church was given as a gift of hope and healing and joy to its community?

One more note about the connection between joy and witness. I believe Luke wants us to connect this passage with one he wrote about earlier. Back in Luke 10, he told us that at the end of their deployment, "the 72" returned filled with joy. The deep joy we long for in our churches and in our personal lives is released when we give ourselves away in ministry to a world that needs to discover Jesus.[47]

What Would it Take?

There may be few other places in the book of Acts where the gap between what happened then and what we experience today is greater. It seems like quite a stretch to think that if we scattered every member of our churches, every one of them would instinctively start introducing new people to Jesus and mobilizing them into new churches.

---

47 Interestingly, this same passage in Luke 10 is the only place in the Gospels where it describes Jesus as filled with joy. In Luke 10.17, "the seventy-two returned with joy." In 10.21, Luke writes, "Jesus, [was] full of joy..." In John 15.11 and 17.13 Jesus speaks of his joy and his desire that it live in us. Hebrews 12.2 says he went to the cross for "the joy set before him." But Luke 10 is the only place the active evidence of his joy is described by observers.

What would it take? What would it take to normalize the frequent multiplication of new churches and large-scale participation in the disciplemaking process that undergirds it? What would it take to shift from thinking about church as gathering to church as going? What would it take to make the deployment of Christians as witnesses the new normal instead of perpetually providing Christians with more theological content?

At the risk of simplicity in the absurd, allow me to suggest five keys to a new normal drawn from the DNA of this account. You might consider these the starting point for a new day of church multiplication.

Don't Wait Until You Feel Ready

No one is ever fully prepared to become a parent. It does not matter whether you planned carefully or were caught by surprise. Becoming a parent is never truly convenient and never something for which you are completely ready. In the same way, it is impossible to appreciate the joy of having a child until you actually have one. I would bet that in the same way, if you had asked the people of the early Jerusalem church if they were ready to be sent out, they would have said, "Not yet."

Those of us in the Western world love to think in linear terms. We like to make plans we can manage in step-by-step increments. We like the notion of graduation at the end of the list—way down the road. We act as if Christians need to master A through Z before we dare send them out to engage a lost world. We are biased to think church planting requires extensive formal training and that an existing church needs to reach a certain size or financial threshold before we can afford to plant another. We hesitate gathering new believers into communities of faith without a seminary-trained leader to oversee them.

I also know that one of the greatest hurdles to planting new churches is fear. Fear that it will be too much work. Fear that it will be too disruptive or expensive for the parent church. Fear that the new church will not succeed. Our human nature loves to avoid risk and therefore we find "reasons" to postpone readiness for a long, long, *long* time.

We can always pursue more training and we can always do more planning. But, the truth is, most of our development comes through on-the-job training. We learn best when we have to apply what we know.

Don't wait until you think you are ready—you will never get there. Step out and watch the Spirit of God show up. Ask yourself, if the decision to scatter the entire Jerusalem church had been yours to make, would you have said yes? Would you have considered them ready? How long has it been since your church sent people out to start a new church?

Start by Making New Disciples
not Church Programs

Remember the childhood rhyme at the beginning of this chapter? As long as we think in terms of buildings and elaborate church programs, we will doubt the timing or advisability of planting a new church. Our predisposition to think and plan in terms of full-service programs and facilities causes a programming bias toward people who are already followers of Christ.

On the contrary, the story of Acts 8 offers a revolutionary approach. Instead of starting by creating programs to gather and equip believers, start with the process of making new disciples out of the harvest. Reach new people. Help them begin following Jesus and then gather them into groups when needed. Only move toward something more formal and structured when those groups start to multiply and reach a critical mass. Fight against the drive for a building until you have so many people that you cannot manage without some kind of dedicated space. Until then, relish the informal and the intimate. By starting this way, every believer can play a major part in launching a new church by focusing on witness rather than church programs. Start by making disciples, not churches.

While this may sound simple, it is actually a quantum shift. A vast majority of church planting efforts over the past twenty-five years have been built on what I would call the core group plus marketing plus rehearsal services approach. While this approach has produced some powerfully influential churches, it is cost and labor intensive. It has also conditioned us to think that starting a church means you have to immediately create the full menu of familiar church programs that will serve Christians in familiar ways.

Start by making disciples out of the harvest and you will discover the freedom to be nimble and creative. Bring hope and healing to people and places of need. Establish "programs" only when necessary to continue developing and deploying the people who start coming to Christ. Avoid the programming beast and you will free up energy to engage the people and community at your doorstep.

THINK PEOPLE GROUPS NOT GEOGRAPHY

Forty years ago Joel Garreau wrote a book, *The Nine Nations of North America*.[48] His premise was that North America is far from a homogeneous place and could be better understood as nine different cultures. My hunch is that were he to write that book today, he might need to title it, *The 900 Nations of North America*.

Not so long ago, my wife and I were walking the pier of downtown Huntington Beach, California. From a distance we noticed a temporary encampment on the beach of tents, high fenced arenas, and vendors. Curious, we moved closer to discover a massive paintball event. Amateurs, pros, equipment reps, autograph seekers, and high-stakes competition filled a long weekend of paint ball nirvana. We stumbled onto an entire subculture of people who love paintball.

That same scenario could be replicated with volleyball players, model airplane hobbyists, NASCAR fans, cyclists, softball fanatics, gym rats, Harley owners, hunters, quilters, fly fishermen, Renaissance Faire devotees, scrapbookers ... you get the idea. People structure their social networks, value systems, and worldviews around those areas of personal interest. These are the tribal units of our modern era—the growing villages that surround us.

---

48 Joel Garreau, *The Nine Nations of North America*. Houghton Mifflin, 1981.

Just because people live on the same street, have the same ethnic heritage, or work in the same industry does not mean they participate in common social-relational subgroups. People connect to one another through work or hobbies or sports or some other common interest. It is a day of increasing tribalism.

With the diversification of culture and the tribal affiliations of people common to the modern day, it is time for church planting to move along tribal as opposed to geographic or ethnic lines alone. It requires learning tribal language, tribal culture, and then contextualizing our methods appropriately. It also means that when we move into these tribes and see new disciples formed, instead of extracting them out of their "tribe" and into an established church, we should help them reach others and plant churches within those groups.

GIVE PEOPLE AWAY
THEY WEREN'T YOURS TO BEGIN WITH

If you participate in planting new churches, you need to be willing to part with some of your people. In fact, you will need to send out some of your best people. And yes, you will feel the relational and financial impact of giving away these leaders.

As a pastor, I felt a personal loss every time one of our leaders moved. We were trying to build ministry capacity and these people were key to making it happen. But at some point, I had to accept the fact that this was not my church and these were not my people. The mission is not my mission. What matters more than my comfort or personal preference is deployment of people into the mission of Jesus. My role is to serve that mission even at the price of giving people away.

Unfortunately, in our bigger-is-better culture, we succumb all too easily to the belief that our significance is found in gathering and holding onto people. Sure, we want the church to be stable. Financial solvency does matter. The long-term relationships we enjoy with people in the church give vibrancy to our sense of community. Nevertheless, when facing a choice between preserving something stable and reaching a lost world, there is no real decision.

By the way, new leaders do not step up until there is a need.

INTEGRATE DEPLOYMENT INTO YOUR DISCIPLESHIP

If we are going to see revolutionary impact on a lost world through the explosive extension of the church, it will require that we rethink discipleship. Church planting begins with making disciples of lost people and a movement of new disciples requires mobilizing disciplemakers.

Following Jesus means joining him where he is going and in what he is about. To be a Christian is to be a disciple who follows Jesus into the world he loves. The term, disciple, is fundamentally a description of relationship between disciple and Rabbi. It describes both lifelong journey and lifelong direction. "Disciple" is not a destination of maturity we arrive at later on, but the very essence of synonym for being a Christian.

Discipleship is ultimately not about the acquisition of biblical facts, compliance with church doctrine, or the cultivation of common religious practices. For too long we have divorced any sense of engagement "out there" from our expectations for a normal Christ-follower. However, the normal expectation for a follower of Jesus "who is scattered" is a disciplemaking life. The pattern of what everyone did in Acts 8 is the pattern of our DNA in action.

Therefore, the environments we develop to shape our people as disciples must include engagement and deployment as much as anything else we do. Jesus said, "Follow me and I will make you fishers of men."[49] Growing a disciple is not something that can be achieved in the sanitary confines of the classroom. Deploying people into the harvest is as much a part of their formation as what happens in the disciplines of solitude. Transform the small groups and/or classes in your church into learning communities that engage a broken world around you as much as they focus on teaching new information.

It's About the Mission *not* More Churches

This may seem like a strange section heading for the conclusion of a chapter on church planting, but the point is that we simply do not need more churches. We don't need more churches if they are trying to fill a gap in our denominational map. We don't need more preaching stations attempting to do church better for Christians who are dissatisfied somewhere else. Those approaches to church planting are not primarily about the harvest but are creating another choice for the sophisticated religious consumer.

---

49 Mark 1.17

We need new churches that will focus on being and bringing good news to more people, more people groups, and more cities. We need more churches that will own their assignment as a missionary force in their community. We need more churches that are formed around making new disciples in new tribal groups in order to reach those tribes. We need more churches that will live to mobilize more people for the fields that are ripe for harvest. By reaching new people for Christ, the planting of new churches should be both normal and frequent.

The big a-ha of Acts 8 is that the starting point for reproducing churches like this is not with an organizational focus on new church development, but with the personal witness and engagement that results in new disciples. It is a process that places the redemption of people and a broken world at the center. It is a process every follower of Christ is made to participate in. It is our DNA. And, it will change the world.

The result is great joy.

seven

Diversity: Heaven in the Present

I looked and there before me was a great multitude that no one could count, from every nation, tribe, people and language, standing before the throne and in front of the Lamb.

They were wearing white robes and were holding palm branches in their hands. And they cried out in a loud voice:

Salvation belongs to our God,
who sits on the throne and to the Lamb.[50]

WHAT if we could taste that reality of heaven in the present? What if the depth of God's heart for all mankind was more than a doctrinal

---

50 Revelation 7.9-11

bullet point but it became the tangible experience of life for his people now? In a world plagued by the injustice of insurmountable divides between people, we follow a Savior who knows no favoritism. So, why the ongoing dissonance between this possibility and our typical reality?

A good friend traveled with me to Kaduna, Nigeria a few years ago to participate in the ordination ceremony of a colleague by the Evangelical Church of West Africa. What an honor. There we were, the only two Westerners in a congregation of more than 1,000 Nigerian faces.

Perhaps you know of the tradition in some African cultures where they dance their way up the aisle when it comes time to give their offerings. I had heard of it, but until this moment, never experienced it. So, when row after row of people stood up to dance their way to the offering basket up front, my friend and I joined in. I thought we held our own—at least without permanent embarrassment. But later, when the denominational leader introduced me to say a few words as a special guest, he could not resist the chance to mention that, as dancers, my friend and I had a lot to learn. Everyone laughed, maybe me most of all. He was right—I will never add dancer to my resume. And no one cared. The entire experience was wonderful.

Why does playful delight over our cultural differences exist as an exception rather than the rule? Of all people, it would seem that as redeemed followers of Christ, our normal experience would be one where diversity strengthens our unity around mission and thus our life in community.

I know that tremendous tribal and cultural tensions persist in Nigeria just as they do in many countries. However, because I live in America, I should write from the perspective of the land I know best. Here in America, Sunday morning at 11:00 a.m. has been described as the most segregated hour of the week. In spite of our heritage as an immigrant nation, our history of racial division continues to find new expressions in our culture as well as the church.

Stewart[51] pastors a church in Kentucky. In his former life he worked as a bouncer in a bar. You will not be surprised that conflict fails to intimidate him. He still stands large and in charge. Yet, to pigeon hole him as brainless muscle would be to do him a great disservice. Stewart embodies a hybrid of courage and compassion that makes him unique as a leader. He exudes strength-based tenderness. And, Stewart is racially color blind.

When we met, Stewart had been the pastor of his church for a few years and was having real success reaching people for Christ. He was ecstatic over the fact that for the first time in their church's history, African-American men and women were coming to Christ and being baptized in increasing numbers. The community was beginning to take notice of the change and was impressed. Unfortunately, some of the folks in his congregation responded with disdain.

One Sunday, after a service that included the baptism of a few African-American men and women, one of the long-standing deacons pulled Stewart aside. Flushed red with anger, this man went nose-to-nose with Stewart.

You can picture the scene: Stewart the former bouncer stood there holding his ground, secure and unmoved, while the deacon spewed venomous arguments with gyrating hand motions. The scene looked something like an irate baseball

---

51 Not his real name.

manager kicking dirt and chest bumping an umpire in the heat of summer.

At the peak of his tirade, in a cleaned-up PG-13 translation, this deacon said, "Pastor, if you don't stop bringing these [insert highly inappropriate racial slur here] into the church, I am going to shove my shotgun where the sun don't shine and blow you away!"

To his credit, Stewart replied with non-anxious humor. "You think I haven't been threatened by people tougher than you? In Christ there is no Jew or Greek or male or female *or white or black*. If that is a problem for you, you should take it up with him."

An extreme example? Certainly.

Unheard of? Hardly.

Left to our human nature, we tend toward bubbles of socio-economic isolation. We choose to associate with people like us. We find comfort with people who look at life the way we do, affirm our opinions, and share our worldview. But, a ghettoized church does not look like the world we are called to reach, and worse, does not reflect the color of God's heart. Jesus was not a blond-haired, blue-eyed, Westerner. Neither was he a champion of our preferred political party. God's mission in the world encompasses every tribe, every people, every nation, and every political persuasion without exception.

It is rather difficult to imagine the local church as a prophetic community demonstrating and declaring God's love for *all* mankind when you hear stories like the one Stewart told me. In a world that excels at prejudice and judgmentalism, you don't need to be a genius to see that a community destined to bring reconciliation might need to live in a different way.

We live in a world where toxic hostility is the norm between people who look or look at life differently. That which divides us runs way beyond issues of race and skin color to include antagonism based on politics, social standing, educational background, types of employment, even sports loyalties. In this cultural climate, I invite you to look afresh at a moment that transformed the church—that transformed us. I invite you to consider letting go of any simplistic thoughts about duty-driven obligation and in their place, imagine the prophetic beauty of unity in diversity. Our DNA as a people who embrace everyone as cherished by God demonstrates a revolutionary message in a polarized world.

A Dream or a Nightmare?

The snowball of change started in an innocuous fashion, but by the time we reach Acts 10, it barrels down the mountain as a fully loaded freight train.

First there were those Grecian Jews who discovered Jesus while in town for the annual Jewish feasts. (Remember the Greek widows in Acts 6?) Then the persecution scattered the church into Samaria and led to Samaritans responding to Jesus. Philip's encounter with the Ethiopian eunuch followed and launched the first foray into the continent of Africa. Meanwhile, other believers scattered further into Roman territory—to places like Antioch and Cyprus and Phoenicia. The fuse of diversity was burning and during an afternoon nap, it would blow.

Eternal significance aside, the events of Acts 10 should make you snicker. While people fussed downstairs over the preparation of a meal, Peter heads up to the roof to pray. The roof provides a bit of privacy and in all likelihood a little breeze as well. While praying, he falls asleep as aromas of meat and bread and Middle Eastern spices waft up from the house and into his dreams.

That makes me laugh. A hungry man, waiting for a meal, falls asleep only to dream of food he cannot eat. This is like someone on a diet dreaming of *Willy Wonka and the Chocolate Factory*. Or, someone who hates fish trapped in a sushi restaurant. You have to stop and enjoy God's sense of humor.

Of course, this was more than a hungry-man fantasizing about food. The Father chose to speak with Peter through a vision that would help him embrace the extent of God's mission far beyond the Jewish world. It was a dream that resulted in the fundamental rewiring of the church's attitude and worldview.

Those of us who are not kosher-keeping Jews might find it tough to connect emotionally with this vision. In principle, we understand that Jewish law forbade eating any of the animals on that lowered sheet. For Peter, this dream was an assault to his sensibilities. These foods were repulsive in ways that go far beyond preference and taste. Obeying Jewish dietary laws was integral to honoring the God of his fathers. By keeping kosher, he demonstrated absolute devotion to his Jewish Messiah. More than tradition or mere custom, avoiding these foods and keeping to the dietary laws distinguished him from everyone who did not follow the one true God. Identity and heritage and godliness were at stake. Peter had never eaten, would never eat, and avoided the homes of anyone who did eat these unclean foods. He would never deny Christ by turning his back on God's laws.

No wonder God repeats the vision three times.

Three times? Does that sound familiar? You could argue that the three-fold pattern of this vision served as divine confirmation for Peter. On the night of Jesus' betrayal, Peter denied knowing Christ three times. Then, in that post-resurrection breakfast at the Sea of Galilee, Jesus reiterates Peter's call to ministry three times. Now, here in a moment that would change the trajectory of the church forever, the Father repeats this vision three times to confirm this is not about being hungry. It was a nap that changed history.

> God has shown me that I should not call any man impure or unclean ... I now realize how true it is that God does not show favoritism but accepts men from every nation who fear him and do what is right.[52]

Just in case the weight of this event has yet to fully grab you, consider two subtle nuances to Luke's report. First, if the only priority was completing the process of Cornelius' conversion to Christ, the Spirit of God could easily have sent someone beside Peter. In case you don't recall, Cornelius was the Roman centurion to whom an angel appeared directing him to send for Peter.[53] Cornelius lived in Caesarea while Peter was 36 miles—two or three days journey—away in Joppa. We know there were other believers there in Caesarea, including

---

52 Acts 10.28, 34-35

53 Acts 10.1-8

Philip who settled there at the end of Acts 8. But, Peter led the Jewish-centered church. Peter stood as the spokesman for Christianity as a Jewish movement more than any other single individual. He was the gatekeeper to a more diverse future. His voice would ring louder than anyone's. And, quite possibly, Peter needed to be converted, too.

A second nuance is revealed by considering the real estate Luke devotes to telling this account. In an era when you could not run to the local Staples™ for another ream of papyrus, every inch of writing surface came at a high price. Yet, this transaction is so significant that Luke tells the whole story twice. He devotes all of Acts 10 and half of chapter 11 to recounting this transformative moment. (That adds up to 66 verses in our contemporary Bible.[54]) Reporting on this one issue occupies more papyrus than the Ascension (3 verses) the entire account of what happened on the Day of Pentecost (41 verses) and the debate about shifting their position on circumcision (21 verses) combined. It would seem that Luke understands how difficult it is to move from a monocultural community to one that celebrates diversity.

A Prophetic Posture

By this point in our walk with Luke through the formative stories of our heritage, radical moments of change like this should no longer surprise us. Yet, at the same time, how do we not find ourselves stunned by the courage of

---

54 It is understood that the verse and chapter conventions were not included in the original, but they form an easy way for us to reference the portions of the text we are discussing.

those early leaders to follow everything the Spirit of God revealed to them?

One of our greatest skills as people is the ability to rationalize. In the church, rationalization often sounds like the spiritualization of our preferences and clever use of Scriptures to sidestep difficult assignments. For his entire life, Peter lived according to what was right. Now, in one afternoon, God changed the rules. Peter could have kept quiet. He could have blamed the whole experience on fatigue or hunger. He could have chosen to challenge his dream with all that he knew of the will of God from the Older Testament. This vision challenged his dedication to obedience and holiness. Gratefully, his willingness to obey and his willingness to be misunderstood carried the day.

That dream and Peter's obedience released a new strand of DNA into our destiny as the Body of Christ. In a prophetic way, this way of life stands in contrast with the persistent hostility of mankind against itself. By the way we embrace people who are different than we are, we interrupt the abusive patterns of the world and put Good News on display.

Jesus unleashes his church as a beacon of hope in a world practiced at intolerance. He commissions us to live out the welcoming embrace of heaven amidst the hellish injustice of the present. To borrow from the music artist Steve Camp, we have the chance to demonstrate, "heaven in the real world." God intends for the church of the present to mirror the diversity of heaven in the future, to reveal the color of his heart for the world.

The heart of God reaches beyond everything that divides men and women. The mission and heart of God obliterates everything we use to marginalize people. The good news of the Gospel reaches far beyond the color of someone's skin or culture to embrace the differences between suburbanites, messy addicts, traditional families, unmarried adults, single moms, Republicans, Democrats, Libertarians, those who went to the right schools, those who didn't finish school, union workers, management leaders, white collar executives, day laborers, those who follow NASCAR, and those who prefer golf.

Again, in Peter's words, "I now realize how true it is that God does not show favoritism but accepts men from every nation who fear him and do what is right."[55]

A community of Christ-followers who embraces men and women of every background without preference makes a bold statement to a dark and hope-hungry world.

Earlier, Jesus said it like this, "By this will all men know you are my disciples, if you love one another."[56] His love is not the kind you can explain because everyone in the room comes from the same cultural cookie cutter of self-reinforcing opinions. When you see a community of radically diverse people whose love for one another cannot be explained, you know something else is at work. Love like this stands out like a flashlight in a pitch-black room.

It is not the church we would have created if left to our own design. Yet, it is exactly the church we need. It is the church the world needs. We were created to declare and demonstrate that this Good News is for all mankind. In a world characterized by prejudice, ostracism, and

---

55 Acts 10.28, 34-35

56 John 13.35

judgmentalism, our DNA makes a revolutionary declaration of eternal value for every person.

Starting Points

Let's not be naïve. This may be the most difficult adjustment in the entire book of Acts and for us. It is one thing to travel to another country and in that context adjust to a different culture for a limited period of time. It is entirely another thing to pursue and embrace people at home that mess with your personal comfort zone.

The pattern of Jesus, the breakthrough for Peter, and the scene in heaven call us to live differently than we would if left to ourselves. So where and how do we get started? Allow me to suggest seven places to begin.

1. Examine Your Rhetoric

One of the first places to start is with your communication patterns. Take a close look at the way you publicly write or speak about other people. Is the language you use inviting and welcoming or does it marginalize people? When you talk about political and social issues, turn down the hostility of your rhetoric toward those who hold different views. Instead, speak of issues, opportunities, and needs. When you talk about meeting needs in your community, avoid the patronizing and labeling language that marginalizes people. Insist that you always speak about people with dignity. The more we adopt us-versus-them language the more we position those who are different than we are as the opposition. One of the most dramatic strategies of Jesus was to move toward those who others saw as unclean.

Conduct an audit of recent church bulletins, newsletters, and other forms of written communication. In addition to looking at ways people have been written about, look for people that might have been omitted. Some churches are so "pro-family" that they communicate second-class status to singles, divorced, or even single parents. The first steps toward more inclusive and welcoming community might actually begin with becoming more sensitive to those sitting in the next row on Sunday morning.

2. Initiate Partnerships in Mission

Our culture sees churches as independent competitors. Kingdom partnerships not only interrupt the confusion about different denominations, they provide a terrific way to demonstrate shared commitment to a community. Find another church or two that embody diversity you do not yet experience and join them. Serve alongside them to meet needs in your community. And, in the process, allow them to increase your understanding and affinity for people in your community who are not part of your congregation.

3. Diversify Your Platform

Ask yourself, how long does it take for someone who comes to your church to see someone who is like them? How much diversity is on display through the people who lead from the front?

I know of a church that is working hard to address the problem that they were aging and losing people in their twenties and early thirties. In spirit, they never meant to shun younger adults, but over the years the age profile of those in leadership and those who were visible on Sunday had simply crept upward. Doing a little assessment, they discovered things like their greeters and ushers were friendly, but all were in their later fifties or sixties. The worship band had only two members below fifty. All the key pastors, all of the elders, and others in significant leadership roles were over fifty. They were good people and good leaders, but inadvertently they made a statement about who the church is for by who stood in places of visibility and leadership. They were also courageous enough to name the problem and aggressively make changes.

One of the quickest and easiest steps toward change is to address the diversity of who stands before your people every week. Consider age, gender, ethnicity, and socio-economic profile. Because communication is predominantly non-verbal, the statements we make by the way we populate the platform, congregational leadership, and the places of public contact make a statement about the kind of people we value most.

4. Pursue Personal Friendships

This is where it gets really simple. Rather than depending on some complex agenda and strategy for organizational change, start by looking at the circle of your friendships. Who do you spend time with that represents a different circle of humanity? Who is within reach that you could begin exploring a deeper relationship with? Are they at work? A client? A neighbor? Someone who shares your favorite hobby or sport? A contact from your child's school, soccer team, or Girl Scout troop?

Nothing changes our personal worldview more than a close personal friend. Just start spending time with someone outside your racial, professional, marital, life stage, or familiar group. Find ways to do life together. They will give you a new lens through which you will view life and priorities and patterns that you can then bring to your congregation. For the church to change, people have to change.

5. Pray for Your Centurion(s)

In much the same way that Jesus spoke about looking for a person of peace, I believe one of the ways a local church can take new ground among people groups is through a bridge builder, a cultural interpreter, a.k.a. your centurion.

Begin praying and fasting and looking for those with whom God might give you favor. Just as Cornelius was a man of broad influence in the region and in the Roman army, ask God to send you a person or a family with deep relationships and personal credibility. Seek someone able to navigate both the cultural dynamics of your present congregation and another segment of humanity around you. When you find them, invite them to become a mentor and coach to your leaders. Give them freedom to shape the way forward.

6. BUILD UNITY AROUND MISSION

Congregations love to talk about unity. It is a Holy Grail of sorts. However, what we typically mean by unity is either the absence of active conflict or a uniformity of common opinion. Real unity is neither one of those. Real unity is the product of shared commitment and sacrifice for a mission that is bigger than we are. Unity is built around our identity in Christ rather than identification with a common lifestyle. It is about alignment with mission, not about avoiding disagreement.

Pursuing people in your community who bring diversity of culture or lifestyle to your congregation will invariably require accommodations by those currently in your church. It requires seeing life through the eyes of someone else. It will call for surrendering personal comfort. Sacrifice like this requires a compelling reason.

God did not interrupt the Jewish dietary system for some altruistic plan of social engineering. It was about his mission to reach a lost and broken world—all of it. He raised the stakes and introduced a new game plan because of people he wanted to reach. If your church is going to reach people beyond your current social norms, it will call for deeper unity and sacrificial alignment around God's mission to reach your entire community.

7. CONFESS AND REPENT

We cannot cheer-lead change into existence. Change demands the courage to behave differently. It calls for courage on another level, too. Below the surface are spiritual strongholds and entrenched biases that can only be broken through spiritual means. Repentance and confession break the grip of both innocent and intentional attitudes toward people who are not like us.

Sometimes these attitudes are expressed forthrightly as happened that day with my friend Stewart. At other times, inappropriate attitudes are expressed with subtle polish. If genuine transformation is to take place, members and leaders alike will need to pause and invite the Spirit of God to reveal the practices, decisions, attitudes, and judgments toward others that call for confession and repentance. This is part of the ongoing redemption of what remains broken in us as people being transformed into the likeness of Christ. It is another place for us to move into the depth of his grace.

On the Other Side of Our Obedience

Peter took six people with him and traveled three days by foot to Caesarea where he discovered the other side of God's orchestrated miracle. His obedience led to the salvation of Cornelius and his entire household. His obedience opened the door for the Gospel to move with power into the Gentile world.

A friend and former colleague summarized this passage for me in a way I have never forgotten: "Lots of people like Cornelius are waiting on the other side of our obedience."[57]

---

57 Terry Fike was a colleague with me at Church Resource Ministries for ten years. He lives in Washington as a man who understands that whether employment is called ministry or carpentry, life in Jesus is a missionary life.

eight
Decision Making and Authority

THINK it is safe to assume that none of us imagine we are committing blasphemy by singing the Doxology. We sing the words all the time. They form one of the most familiar strands in our global worship tapestry.

> Praise God from whom all blessings flow;
> Praise Him all creatures here below ...

The Doxology, as we know it today, must be the furthest thing from inappropriate worship we can imagine. However, at the time it was written, common opinion in the church held that only words from the Psalms should be sung as hymns in the church. To write and sing lyrics composed of other words felt like adding to the inspired canon of Scripture. It was blasphemous and sinful.

In this religious climate, Thomas Ken had the audacity to pen the words of a hymn whose final stanza we now know as The Doxology. Ken, an Anglican minister and later a bishop, published this and several hymns for the boys of Winchester College in 1674, instructing them to use these hymns in their private devotions.[58]

I find stories like this fascinating, even a bit humorous. Something we now hold as highly traditional was originally inappropriate, possibly seditious. Back in the day, Ken's action would have raised serious objections. So, it is fair to ask, who or what gave him the authority to go against established conviction? What gave him the right to instruct young men to worship in a manner that church tradition held as sinful? For that matter, when does any individual or group of believers have the right to do what a majority has never done before?

The same scenario repeats in the later 19th century. William Booth, the founder of the Salvation Army, started holding church services in storefront facilities that looked nothing like church buildings. He went on to raise the ire of good Christian folk in England by writing "Christian" words to popular tunes, playing the music on non-approved instruments, dressing his people in military-like uniforms, and doing all of this on public street corners. What kind of excuse is it to say, "Why should the devil have all the good

---

58 www.cyberhymnal.org, article on the hymn: "Awake, My Soul, and with the Sun"

music?"[59] How dare he encourage a movement representing the cause of Christ in ways that many saw as wrong? Who gave him the authority to make decisions like that?

In recent decades, wave after wave of reactions just like this washed through the Christian community in response to new ministry approaches in the church. When ex-hippies in the Jesus People era started coming to church in sandals and extremely casual clothes, many reacted that they were being disrespectful, forgetting to "fear of the Lord." When churches stopped having Sunday evening services, many wondered if they were compromising their dedication to Christ. When churches started adding Saturday evening services, many questioned whether non-Sunday services could ever be considered appropriate weekly worship. When extensive use of video and drama became normal, some wondered if we had compromised on the centrality of the written Word. The trend continues as local churches learn to contextualize their methods for the sake of our mission. New approaches often rub against the grain of long-established tradition.

So, when does a body of believers or a ministry leadership team have the authority to do something of which the larger Christian community would not approve? When is it right to start or stop something that would contrast with the broader canon of best practice? Answering these questions does not merely provide help for the big pioneering decisions, but actually informs the way daily decision making and leadership happen every day.

---

59   Steve Addison at, movements.net identifies the source of this statement as January 22, 1882 at the theatre in Worcester. After hearing one song, Booth asked his hosts, "What tune was that?" That's "Champagne Charlie is my name". "That's settled it," William Booth decided as he turned to his son Bramwell. "Why should the devil have all the best tunes?"

Until this point in our "conversation with the early church," the turning points we have examined were rather obvious and dramatic. This next one is recorded in a much subtler way. In fact, it almost sneaks by unnoticed. Nonetheless, the implications of this next development are anything but subtle.

The Center of Gravity Shifted

From day one, life in the early church orbited around Jerusalem under the leadership of the apostles. Even when the persecution of Acts 8 scattered the entire church, the apostles hung on in Jerusalem and gave leadership to new developments from there. For example, when Samaritans started coming to Christ in significant numbers, the apostles delegated Peter and John to go check things out. And, when word got to Jerusalem that there was a great response to the Gospel in Antioch, the apostles appointed Barnabas to go and support what was taking place there. Bottom line, before Acts 13, the center of gravity for the church was anchored in Jerusalem. After the events of Acts 13, everything shifted.

> While they were worshipping the Lord and fasting, the Holy Spirit said, "Set apart for me Barnabas and Saul for the work to which I have called them." So, after they had fasted and prayed, they placed their hands on them and sent them off.[60]

---

60 Acts 13.2-3

Our familiarity with the history of the Church in the New Testament makes it easy to take the missionary journeys of Paul and Barnabas for granted. However, the decision to send off these two missionaries was anything but benign. The implications of what Luke describes in two simple sentences launched revolutionary shifts in the global Christian movement that still affect us today.

We shifted geographically. Until this moment, Christianity was a regional presence on the eastern edges of the Mediterranean. After deploying these first missionaries, that regional movement exploded across the Roman world. We shifted culturally. The sending of Barnabas and Saul launched us from a movement with a strong Jewish bias into one of multicultural diversity. We have never looked back. Today we fully embrace every tribe, every nation, and every people group as equally loved and equally pursued by the heart of God.

On that day we also shifted from a pattern of accidental expansion to intentional pursuit of an unreached world. Look at the maps in the back of your Bible and I bet you will find one that highlights the missionary journeys of Paul. The formal appointment and commissioning of missionaries was so significant that we have collectively marked the first three missionary journeys as something worthy of permanent study. Today, we almost take the global missions enterprise for granted. Until that moment in Antioch, formally deployed cross-cultural missionaries had never existed. These actions forged our DNA as a local-global enterprise.

The actions of this local congregation were revolutionary. And precisely because of the watershed of implications from this decision, the one thing they did not do should startle us. The fact that those leaders in Antioch made no attempt to consult with, get approval from, or even inform the apostles in Jerusalem before they acted is stunning. This local church sent these men out as emissaries of Christ and his larger movement without a commission from established leadership.

What gave them the authority, not to mention the audacity, to make and act on such a decision? What gave them the right to do something that could shape the perception of Christianity throughout the Roman Empire? Who gave them the authority to send these two men on a potentially life-threatening journey? Had they considered all the pitfalls and precedents?

In addition to the local-global implications of the moment, the decision to launch this new enterprise signifies a shift in the decision making authority entrusted to a local body of believers. When the leadership team of that Antioch church recognized the prompting of the Holy Spirit they understood their responsibility to respond in immediate obedience. When they laid hands on Barnabas and Saul during their send-off ceremony, they demonstrated the authority to perform the spiritual tasks of commissioning, blessing, and ministry appointment. The act of laying on hands is both a symbolic and a spiritual transaction. Only the apostles in Jerusalem had exercised such authority until now.

I recognize that the local-global mission of the church is a major theme of this passage. For the sake of focus, I will return to the subject of our local-global assignment in the final chapter of this book. In this chapter we will focus in on the revolutionary nature of decision making and authority entrusted to every community of believers as they seek to carry out the mission of Jesus.

Our DNA: Listen and Obey

The matter-of-factness by which Luke reports those events in Antioch paints a stark contrast to the way we make big decisions in the church these days. While we ponder and debate and drill down on the policies and precedents of a decision like this, they didn't seem to do anything of the sort. I could paraphrase Luke's report this way: "The Holy Spirit said we should send them out, so we sent them out. How could we do otherwise? And, by the way, since it was a matter of obedience, we acted right away."

Life as his church does not mean following a punch list of religious patterns, programs, traditions, and constraints. It is a high-risk adventure of faith as the Spirit guides us into the fullness of the life and mission of Jesus. Leadership is more than wise planning executed by competent individuals—there is always another player in the room. His direction is what matters most. As a result, serving as a leader in the body of Christ should be a constant adventure of following the dynamic leadership of the Spirit.

Listening and obeying are not only fundamental to following Jesus personally—they define the essence of daily practice for the community of leaders who are entrusted with the responsibility for shepherding a local church. Paul's admonition that we walk in step with the Spirit applies to the way we live as a community just as much as it does to us individually.[61]

In Acts 1, Jesus told his disciples to wait in Jerusalem for the promised Holy Spirit.[62] The promised Spirit of God is our counselor, the one who guides us into all truth.[63] Day in and day out the Good Shepherd calls his sheep by name and leads them out.[64] Jesus' commitment is to live among his people and lead them through his Spirit. He does not serve merely as an iconic figurehead of the church, but as the active leader of his people.[65] He is the one who calls to, speaks to, directs, provokes, whispers, guides, and empowers his people. He leads and we follow.

This strand of our DNA means that both the challenge and the adventure for every body of believers are to listen and follow the direction of the Spirit. Superseding church polity, precedents of tradition, or even the personal preferences of established leadership, the essence of decision making boils down to seeking and following his leadership. We can trust him to lead us. The truth is, he loves to speak to us far more than we like to listen.

The practice of listening-obeying obliterates any notion of church life as a static experience of religious ritual. We should anticipate the specific and contextually relevant direction of the Spirit as normal life. We should be on the

---

61 Galatians 5.25

62 Acts 1.4-5

63 John 14.25-26

64 See John 10

65 Colossians 1.18, 2.10, 2.19

lookout for his prompting to try what we have never tried before. We should expect him to suggest new approaches that just might extend our impact in the world. Just as the Holy Spirit spoke to the church in Antioch and asked them to deploy Barnabas and Saul in a way no one had ever done before, he continues to lead his people to take new steps that will radically advance the mission of Jesus in our contemporary world.

This discipline of following the leadership of the Spirit could challenge the way we practice leadership in the church. On the one hand, it means that a core responsibility of church leadership is the disciplined practice of listening for, attending to, and implementing the directives of the Spirit. On the other hand, it means cultivating the same posture of listening, discerning, and obeying the Spirit's leading among the congregation. Pastors and other congregational leaders do not hold a corner on the market of direction or wisdom from God. The wind blows where it will and no one sees from where it is coming. Imagine a local congregation that seeks the Spirit's direction instead of wrangling over differing personal opinions.

Living into the reality of this DNA could change the way congregational business happens, too. *Robert's Rules of Order* provides a helpful process for creating orderly meetings, but what if there was something more important than order? What if the whole congregation learned to listen for and follow the direction of the Spirit together? The practice of waiting on and listening for the leadership of the Spirit will transform the way they gather to address the "business" of the church body.

So, how do we live into our DNA as a listening and responding community? There is a tremendous heritage in Christendom regarding the processes of discernment and listening prayer, but right here in this passage, Luke reveals a great deal about how we might get started.

Leadership as a Discernment Community

First of all, let's admit what we do not know. Luke told us that the Holy Spirit "said" they were to set apart Barnabas and Saul. Luke did not tell us *how* they "heard" him speak. Did the Spirit speak out loud in a voice everyone heard? Did he supernaturally cause words to appear on the wall where they were meeting? Could it have been a simple suggestion from an astute teenager that everyone recognized as something far more? We do not know how the Holy Spirit spoke, but we do know the context in which he spoke.

Luke sets the stage for this big moment by naming the leadership team—five prophets and teachers—in the church at Antioch.[66] He then completes the context by showing us that these leaders were worshipping and fasting together at the time the Holy Spirit spoke to them.

We'll consider their behavior together in a moment, but before diving into the details, we need to stop and take notice of the fact that they were doing this together. The context in which the Holy Spirit spoke was one where leaders were working and worshipping together in community. It echoes

---

66 Acts 13.1: The five mentioned include Barnabas, Simeon called Niger, Lucius of Cyrene, Manaen, and Saul.

back to Acts 1 when the nature of leadership in community was first named during the selection of Matthias.[67]

The posture of this leadership team demonstrates what preparation for discernment looks like. Granted, the Holy Spirit can speak at any time and in any way he wishes, but there are ways that a leadership community, a ministry team, or an entire congregation can cultivate attentiveness. When we look closely at the behavior of those leaders in Antioch, we find four factors that attuned their ears to listen for the Spirit's leadership.

THE DISCIPLINES OF WORSHIP AND FASTING

It is not incidental that these leaders in Antioch were worshipping and fasting when they heard the Spirit tell them to set aside Barnabas and Saul. It is also interesting that Luke describes their behavior in what seems to be a matter-of-fact manner. Fasting and worship are mentioned as if this is what leaders do all the time. The nature of their worship is undefined and the focus or duration of their fasting is unnamed.

In the twenty-first century church in the West, worship generally means a gathering of believers where music is the dominant activity. I do not believe we can make that assumption here. The word that the NIV translates as worship has a strong bias toward service or ministry activity.[68] At the

---

67 Acts 1.21-26

68 *Latreuo* means to serve, minister, to perform an act of worship. It is the word used at the end of Romans 12.1 when Paul wrote, "I urge you, in view of God's mercy, to offer up your bodies as living sacrifices ... this is your reasonable act of *service*," (or *worship*, in some translations.)

very least, Luke's point is that these leaders were actively engaged together, serving the Lord as an act of worship. They did much more than process decisions in the boardroom; they sought and served the Lord together.

And, they fasted together. It begs the question, how often do most pastoral staff teams or church governing boards fast together? My observation is that fasting as a deliberate practice among leaders is usually relegated to times of crisis or major decision. However, the discipline of fasting and the focused prayer that accompanies it enhances our growth as leaders able to discern the Spirit's leading.

Sure, the Holy Spirit is fully capable of breaking through the clutter of our busyness and dialogue at any time. But, that is the problem. He needs to break through. The practice of fasting and worshiping together not only clears the clutter, but it moves us into a posture of dependence and attentiveness. Engaging the Father through worship and fasting might be one of the most strategic pathways leaders can follow. The life of a church community that listens for and follows the leading of the Spirit begins with leaders who will attune themselves through these disciplines of dependence.

THE PRACTICE OF LISTENING

Listening for the leading of the Spirit is not a formula. There are no simple steps or magic codes. Listening is a matter of paying attention. The problem is we are simply too busy talking to notice God is trying to get our attention. Whether speaking of our personal lives or our life as the church, dedicated time for quiet and reflection are pretty rare. We fear silence. We avoid what the radio and television industry call "dead air." We prefer tightly scripted worship services and we become driven to get everything done on our business meeting agendas. Listening often starts with turning down the noise and, well, listening.

God loves to speak and he uses a wide variety of ways to do so. In Scripture we see him speaking through visions, by angelic intervention, in dreams, at a burning bush, with handwriting on the wall, through the rushing wind, and in the still small voice of the Spirit. He speaks through the direct testimony of his Word and in the subtle promptings that accompany prayer. In local congregations he might speak through a specific passage of Scripture, the seasoned wisdom of an elder, the innocent question of a child, or even the caustic voice of a critic. Our experience brings Jesus' words in John 10 to life. The Good Shepherd constantly speaks and calls out to his sheep.

I frequently help local congregations with some aspect of strategic planning as a way to address the challenges and opportunities of the future. What I have learned is that appropriate congregational planning is fundamentally a process of listening for and aligning ourselves with the leading of the Spirit. Far from any sort of humanly clever planning process, strategic planning is really a spiritually empowered discernment process. The same principle holds true for every decision, discussion, ministry update, and planning session. Every phase of leadership activity is an opportunity to listen afresh for the leading of the Spirit.

As you start listening more intentionally, pay attention to the quiet and contrary voices. They are often available to hear from the Spirit because they are least vested in whatever proposal is driving the conversation.

RESPONSIVE OBEDIENCE

Obedience is often expensive. By expensive, I do not mean that there is not a great return on our obedience, but that before a return comes in, what we experience is the price of change. Perhaps you already noticed this, but when the Spirit told them to send off Barnabas and Saul, he was asking this congregation to make a profound sacrifice. Barnabas was effectively their senior pastor, having been appointed by the apostles in Jerusalem. Saul was the prominent rising star of new leadership. Together, these two formed the bookends of their pastoral leadership team. Sending them off would create a massive hole in the life and leadership of this congregation. Yet, the church acted without hesitation or regret. Every indication in the passage says they acted immediately.

Responsive obedience is like that. Not only does it mean an eagerness to hear from God, but also includes a commitment to obey whatever the Spirit says. In practice, this is like signing a blank check and inviting the Lord to fill in anything he chooses. This posture of responsive obedience is how we soften our hearts to become more attentive to the leading of the Spirit. It is entirely the opposite of the response mentioned by the author of Hebrews when he said, "Today if you hear God's voice, do not harden your hearts."[69]

OPENNESS TO WHAT IS NEW

An emphasis on listening for the Spirit's leading invites a fresh way of thinking about leadership in the church. Leadership is not about having perfect plans or flawless

---

69 Hebrews 3.7, 15; 4.7; see also Psalms 95.7-8.

wisdom, but about working as stewards entrusted with the assignment to help the body follow the head who is Christ. And, it is a posture of responsive obedience which includes being open to what is new, unknown, or untried. Without an openness to what might be new, we live with filters that only reinforce what already exists. Without openness to something untried, Barnabas and Saul might have stayed in Antioch serving the church there.

This kind of openness is revolutionary for organizational life. The nature of organizations is to preserve status quo, avoid risk, move toward the lowest common denominator, and choose a path that ruffles the fewest feathers. Adopting a posture of willingness to step into new territory any time the Spirit chooses to speak is a pathway to an adventurous, at times risk-tasking, journey of dependence.

For those leaders in the Antioch church, this was a step into the unknown. Prior to this moment in human history, formally commissioned missionaries had never been conceived of, let alone sent out by a local congregation.

No one knew what might be possible until men like Thomas Ken started writing new lyrics for worship songs ... Until William Booth established brass bands and storefront churches ... Until the American Sunday School Union started establishing Sunday Schools as a church planting strategy across the western frontier ... Until missionary societies formed in Europe to send and support bands of missionaries around the globe ... Until the house church movement in China erupted when traditional missionaries were kicked out ...

It makes me wonder, what have we not thought of yet that might result in radical kingdom advancement? What new approaches have not been tried regarding worship, buildings, community engagement, discipleship, leadership structures, evangelism, kingdom partnerships, etc.? We have no idea what might be possible today as the Spirit of God continues to lead those who will listen and obey.

The question for all of us is whether we are listening and open to follow wherever he may lead. He may not lead you to do something that appears revolutionary, but that is not the point. The point is that our DNA as his church calls us to listen and obey the direction of the Spirit. Following Jesus together as a community is a revolutionary life of adventure following the leadership of the Spirit.

Whether he invites you to take steps that seem simple and small or steps that are scary and sacrificial, the real question is the same. Will you listen and obey, even if he asks you to try something never done before?

nine

Contextualization and Courage

A **FEW** years ago, my daughter and I attended the matinee showing of a blockbuster 3-D movie. Part science fiction, part fantasy, part epic mythology, and mostly special effects, it was an engaging but easily forgotten entertainment experience. However, we will never forget what happened midway through the film. There we sat, adorned with dorky disposable 3-D glasses in the midst of a silent theatre audience. Hundreds of us were fixated on the intensity of a mythical battle scene when, suddenly, the theater started shaking. For a moment this new sensory effect took our 3-D experience into a 4-D zone. The synchronization of the movement we felt with the scene on the screen made me think this was the introduction of a new type of special effects. But, it wasn't the building shaking—it was the earth beneath us.

Earthquakes are familiar territory for those living in California. Small ones that no one feels happen all the time. Bigger ones do not happen very often, but long-time residents can distinguish different types. This one was a big roller undulating up and down, amplified, I am sure, by our location four stories above the ground.

The previously entranced audience transformed immediately into a highly animated mob. As if on cue, the entire theatre erupted in agitated conversation about what we should do, whether this was "the big one," and how long the quake was lasting. Many remained glued to their seats. Quite a few jumped up and started running toward the exit.

At the peak of pandemonium, a lone voice in the crowd yelled out, *"Hey! I'm a structural engineer. Stop running in the dark! You are safer if you stay put!"*

Then, another patron—one obviously acclimated to earthquakes—shouted back, *"Everyone, please shut up! I am trying to watch the movie!"*

My point is this, we live in the midst of seismic change that affects every aspect of life—the church included. Our response to the destabilization of change mirrors what took place inside that theater. *Everyone* is affected by and talking about the tremors of change. Some are particularly unsettled, others desperately fight to make the shaking stop, some act surprisingly calm, and more than few appear to be nonplussed spectators looking for entertainment to assuage the uncertainties of reality.

Change is like that. It is like that for us as individuals and it is like that for us as the church. The very moments that are pregnant with opportunity paralyze us with the discomfort of their uncertainty.

So, we should not be surprised that this era of global change has unleashed a conversation about the very nature of the church. On every continent, ministry leaders explore questions about the nature, mission, effectiveness, and contextual relevance of the church in its current forms. Some are pioneering new forms of gathering as the Body of Christ. Others experiment with new ways to engage the needs of the culture around us. The sheer magnitude of fresh ideas and contemporary writing about the church is nothing less than an ecclesiological Niagara Falls.

In all this wrestling over possibilities and new strategies for the church, questions arise over what is appropriate and what is simply going too far.

How many times have you been part of a conversation or congregational meeting where people debated whether this or that change meant inappropriate compromise or that we were becoming like the world? How far should we go in adapting our methods in order to connect with our culture? What types of changes are acceptable and what should never be changed? What does "living in the world, but not of the world" mean for our methods and approaches as a church? When have we crossed the line? How far is too far?

Throughout this journey with the early church, we have seen that time and time again they were sent back to the drawing board to determine how they needed to adapt in order to continue moving forward. In Acts 15, we come to what might have been the most complicated moment of all. Depending on your perspective, the scope of the change they made here could be either the most encouraging or most deeply disturbing chapter in the story of the first century church.

Anatomy of a Debate

Luke says a debate erupted when some men from Judea traveled to Antioch and started teaching on the necessity of circumcision. Although he says it created a "sharp dispute and debate,"[70] he holds back on a host of details. I am curious, who were these men? Was there anyone of significance? Where and how did the debate take place? Was this something big and dramatic or the back office dispute of a few? I realize that my curiosities will have to remain unanswered. But, I also realize that by leaving details like this out of the story, Luke does what he has done so often and narrows our attention to the essence of the issue and its watershed of implications.

Most of us reading this passage in the twenty-first century have a hard time relating to the question of circumcision as an emotionally charged crisis. For one thing, the issue was resolved way back then. For another, since we did not grow up in first century Israel, we don't empathize with the importance of maintaining our Jewish identity during an era of military occupation. But, for those leaders at that point in history, this question is huge.

Is salvation by faith alone or are there other requirements that must be met? Specifically, does a man who becomes a follower of Jesus have to be circumcised before he is saved?

---

70 Acts 15.1-2

Or, to frame it another way, does someone have to become a Jew before they can become follower of Jesus? Circumcision has been the sign of God's covenant people since the days of Abraham, so what makes us think it should change now?

In Antioch, these questions were more than matters of theological clarity. This was personal. As a coastal city and trading center, the location of Antioch, in modern day Syria, positioned this church to reach much more than diasporate Jews. If you were one of the scores of new gentile believers in Antioch,[71] these teachers were telling you that you were not really saved. Your devotion to Christ was in question. And, if this new teaching was true, you and a host of others would all have to be circumcised.

As the cause of Christ expanded further throughout the Roman world, Jewish believers must have struggled with the feeling that their heritage was slipping away. Christianity grew out of Jewish roots and was still seen as a Jewish sect. However, success in reaching non-Jews brought change to everything that was historically meaningful. New believers poured into the church without intrinsic appreciation for the Jewish feasts, kosher laws, or even the meaningful music of the synagogue. Surely, someone must draw a line in the sand at some point. Should we not set a limit as to how much could or should be changed to accommodate outsiders?

Most of us have had enough experience that we can understand the ethos of their tension. Our relationship with

---

71 We know the Barnabas was sent to Antioch by the elders in Jerusalem because the church was exploding there. As a Levite from Cyprus, Barnabas' bi-cultural heritage was certainly a factor in what must have been a growing multicultural congregation. We are never told how many people were coming to Christ, but by this time it is safe to assume that we are not just talking about dozens, but hundreds of new Christ-followers.

God and our experience of his presence intertwines with the practices and traditions of our church life. Certain forms of worship and patterns of life that we learned to cherish during our young adulthood or the early years after we came to Christ will always be the most meaningful. In some cases, the forms of our Christian experience feel inseparable from our theology.

When our preferred pattern of church life changes we grieve the loss. When the style of our worship gatherings are altered it feels like the substance of our faith is compromised. When the music that leads us into the presence of the Father most meaningfully gets tossed for some new style we don't appreciate, it is easy to believe that something irreplaceable was lost. Yes, we understand that the forms we find meaningful and the substance of our faith are not the same thing. But, they often feel inextricable.

The question of circumcision raised all of these sensibilities for the Jewish believers of the first century. It also touched profound questions about how we should respond to changing context and culture without compromising the historical faith expressed through established tradition. With so much at stake, the church in Antioch asked a group of people to travel more than 300 miles by foot to Jerusalem to sort it all out.

Contextualization Done Right

Stories are more fun to tell and more fun to read when there is a big mystery to be solved. In this case, we know the outcome, so there is no suspenseful buildup to a big reveal. We know they decided that Gentiles do not have to be circumcised. Therefore, our challenge is to look deeper into the nooks and crannies of their rationale in order to discover principles that will guide us when we need to contextualize our methods and strategies to reach a changing world. The decision they made shows us that sometimes making a bold change can be the best way to advance the Gospel. At the same time, the reasoning behind their decision gives us a lens through which we might see our own way forward.

Consider decisions your church struggled over recently. Perhaps you wrestled with the question of sending people out to start another church, making significant change to your weekend ministry schedule, embarking on a significant building-related project, shutting down a historically meaningful program, changing the style or approach of your worship services in a substantial way, ...the list could go on and on.

I heard the story of a local church that chose to move their weekend worship gathering to Saturday night. They did not just add a Saturday service, they closed down their Sunday gathering entirely and only met on Saturday. They made the shift in order to take advantage of the fact that their building (an old movie theater) was located right in the middle of the main club scene in town. On any Saturday night, this main drag swarmed with people. By choosing to meet when and where people were hanging out, they were placing themselves right in the middle of the action. It was a bold move aimed at reaching people for Christ who literally gathered at their doorstep. And, it paid off even though a segment of the congregation struggled with the change. Some felt the church was forsaking our Christian heritage by abandoning the first day of the week. Others found the change of longstanding weekend rhythms simply discomforting. But I don't write of this example in order to dissect it.

I would like you to consider the decision of that Jerusalem council in light of a real world example like this that you might be able to relate to. Keep this church's shift in the back of your mind—unless you have a better one of your own—as you consider five principles demonstrated by our forefathers as they grappled with the future of circumcision.

MISSION TRUMPS TRADITION

On the one hand, circumcision predates Israel as the sign of God's covenant people. On the other hand, men and women from a wide swath of humanity were now coming to Christ and confirmed in that faith by the familiar work of the Spirit.

> God who knows the heart, showed that he accepted them by giving the Holy Spirit to them, just as he did to us. He made no distinction between us and them, for he purified their hearts by faith.[72]

The situation forced a foundation-shaking question. Although God is doing something new, does this new movement really require a change in something as historically significant as circumcision? And, even if we consider the possibility of change, what should guide our decision making?

---

72 Acts 15.8-9

Ultimately, what is at stake in this moment, as in so many of the DNA shaping moments in Acts, is the mission that has been at the core of our DNA since day one. The predominant questions in a moment like this are not questions about tradition or preferences, but questions about how we might extend the Gospel among people who do not know or appreciate those traditions. God is a missionary God with a global agenda and we serve that agenda. It means that, when the world we are trying to reach changes, we must have the courage to put our mission first. This is a defining distinction. Our assignment is not to be curators of a museum that preserves the traditions and culture of the church as we knew it. We are to be missiologists who study the nuances of our context and adapt our methodologies in order to more effectively reach the people surrounding us.

Our mission is based on the fact that "through the grace of the Lord Jesus we are saved,"[73] not through conformity to any religious customs or laws.

The cross of Christ is a legitimate stumbling block[74] which is not open for compromise, but there is no merit to adding another "yoke"[75] that might get in the way. As James said at the end of this meeting, "We should not make it difficult for the Gentiles who are turning to God."[76] Or, to put it into the positive, we should do everything we can to remove every obstacle we can so that we might reach as many as we can for Christ.

---

73 Acts 15.11

74 1 Corinthians 1.18-25

75 Acts 15.10

76 Acts 15.19

UNCERTAINTY IS CERTAIN

Every leader would love to stand before a congregation with the ability to say without doubt, "Thus says the Lord." Look, we have these tablets of stone written in his own hand and you can read them for yourself. Or, apart from tablets of stone, we would like some version of "we saw the finger of God writing his plan across the walls of the church building."

The desire for certainty runs deep in all of us. We would love to know that the results of our decisions are guaranteed, especially when we stand before others to explain those decisions. Unfortunately, the task of leadership usually begins with the surrender of our quest for certainty and our longing to control the outcomes of our decisions. Obedience is about faith. Leadership means trusting the One who guides us more than we trust the quality and detail of our plans.

"After much discussion," Peter, Paul, Barnabas, and James brought clarity to the group.[77] They told stories about how God showed up in miraculous ways to confirm his work among the Gentiles. They connected their present experience with the words of the prophets. And then they made a proposal. The wording of that proposal and the description of the group decision is fascinating.

James does *not* say, "God has spoken," or, "It is clear that God is charting a new course and circumcision is no longer necessary." Instead, he offers a personal opinion: "It is my judgment, therefore, that we should not make it difficult for the Gentiles who are turning to God."[78]

---

77 Acts 15.7-21

78 Acts 15.19

Or even more fascinating, the description of group approval was that "it seemed good..."[79] The group decision was not wrapped in language of certainty or divine decree, but with that tenuous sense that this seemed like a good idea. Thousands of years of God-defined tradition were set aside on the basis of a plan that just made sense.

I would have thought that a decision of this magnitude would be wrapped in a narrative about how they prayed and fasted and waited on the Lord for specific direction. But that is not the way Luke reports it. They embraced the fact that this was the best they knew and the best way they had to remove an impediment to the expansion of the gospel throughout the world. They trusted the Holy Spirit had been at work, not only by showing his presence among the Gentiles, but also by guiding them toward a decision.

DEBATE AND DIFFERENCES ARE A STRENGTH

The way the council in Jerusalem processed this decision offers a powerful lesson that stands in contrast to the common behavior of most local churches. Arriving at this decision was a process of serious debate. Anytime we look to contextualize ministry for a changing world, taking the pathway through differing opinions can help us get to a place of better wisdom.

Luke does not tell us how long they met, but he does tell us about the intensity of their dialogue. He framed the whole chapter by introducing it as a "sharp dispute and

---

79 Acts 15.28

debate."[80] He repeats that emphasis when he talks about the meeting of the apostles and elders telling us they had, "much discussion," or what could be translated, "great debate."[81]

How are decisions made among the leaders you know? How often are differing opinions solicited and considered? How well have people learned to disagree on principle without making it personal? Looking at this passage we see that the group of Pharisees who had come to Christ were arguing not just for circumcision, they wanted to require new converts to obey the laws of Moses. It is a classic case of issue expansion, but it is also a testimony to the fact that this was a room filled with diverging opinions.

Most congregations cringe in fear at the thought of strong differing opinions as if they were an unavoidable threat to unity. However, unity means choosing to move forward together after coming to a decision. Unity is not a matter of uniform opinion but united action. Inviting those with divergent opinions into the conversation may make things messier, but it opens the dialogue to all the nuances that need to be considered. Close down the conversation to those who are already of like mind and you very likely close yourself to something the Spirit would like to say through the larger Body of Christ.

EXPECT THE DISSONANCE OF CHANGE

I like to tease that the church wrote the book on the seven last words of change: *We've never done it that way before.*

---

80 Acts 15.2

81 Acts 15.7

Sure, the church does not have a corner on the problem; it is common to the human condition. Resistance to change is endemic to every human organization. As a result, even the right change carried out in the best possible way creates dissonance for people. Leaders need to be prepared and they need to be wise. Managing change well means stewarding people well as they deal with the effects caused by our changes.

One of the more destabilizing facets of our common response to change is that when new approaches are proposed as a way to increase effectiveness, those changes are experienced as an indictment on the past. People who have been highly vested in creating or sustaining the former ways hear the arguments for new ways as a criticism of what they hold dear, a devaluing of what they sacrificed to build.

For example, the Sunday evening service was a mainstay in congregational life since the days that church buildings were the first places in town to have electricity. Today, most places find it hard to maintain the Sunday evening service. Does that mean those who canceled Sunday evening services were compromising the faith of our fathers or criticizing those who loved that practice? When culture and context change, our methods and ministry strategies need to be re-examined. New approaches today are not an indictment on what worked in a different era.

Look closely at one facet of what those early leaders did and you find a wise response. At the very moment when they were taking a radical step regarding circumcision, they found a way to honor the convictions of those who would feel most uneasy about this change. In the instructions sent out to the churches, they included a way to honor the past. They asked people "to stay away from food offered to idols.…

because Moses has been preached..."[82] While charting a new way forward, they found a way to respect the older ways. They even connected it to Moses, without getting tangled up in the Mosaic law argument.

Because we live in a world that is constantly changing and because we are always learning more of what it means to follow Christ, there must always be adaptations and adjustments to the way we do life together as the Body of Christ. So, in this light, allow me to suggest that even these instructions about avoiding food offered to idols were temporary. They were only an intermediate step in contextualizing their mission. We never see the argument for avoiding food offered to idols repeated in the same way. By the time we get to Paul's letter to the Corinthians, he argues that we have freedom to eat food offered to idols, because an idol is nothing.[83]

Becoming Missiologists

The larger lesson of Acts 15 is that ministry leaders need to live as missiologists who lead the way in studying and adapting to reach a changing culture. Our job as leaders is to translate the Gospel and the forms through which it is expressed into every context in ways that "do not make it difficult for [those] who are turning to God." Leaders are called to champion the dynamic process of courageous contextualization in order to advance the Gospel. The Gospel

---

82   Acts 15.20-21, 29

83   1 Corinthians 8.1-13. (Cf. Romans 14, especially v. 19-21.)

is good news for all mankind in all nations from all tribes at all times.

Missiologists are students of culture. Missiology takes a scientific approach to the study of what it takes to fulfill our mission in a complex global environment. Missiologists examine language, values, art, and the forms of communication that make cultures and people groups unique. They place the people who need to be reached above the biases and personal preferences they bring to the conversation. Like most scientists, they are willing to hold ideas loosely while they test them. And, they are willing to be wrong as they continue to learn.

In the complex cultural landscape of the twenty-first century, pastors and ministry leaders must become missiologists. We cannot afford to be chaplains of a Christian heritage anchored in a culture that no longer exists. We need to lead the church to engage our culture effectively. Leading this way means learning to communicate our message and contextualize our methods in new ways for which we were never trained. It means our seminaries are going to have to put missiological training at the heart of all pastoral training. And, it means taking the risk to tinker with what is familiar and known and trusted in order to discover what would be more effective.

If the church of the first century was right to set aside circumcision in order to serve the advancement of the Gospel, then none of our current forms or styles of doing ministry are non-negotiable. None of the ways we do church hold a candle to the longevity or God-appointed stature of circumcision. Change for the sake of change is not the goal, but then avoiding change because it is risky and difficult has no merit either.

Acts 15 is missiology in action. Our DNA as a missionary people entrusted with a redemptive mandate calls the leaders of every generation in every context to find the courage to adapt and adopt the methods that will most effectively reach the world surrounding them.

It is Time for Dancing

Patrick is one of the most amazing and inviting leaders I have ever met. He pastors a church in Nairobi, Kenya. In fact, he is the first Kenyan pastor of a church planted and originally pastored by missionaries a few decades ago. Patrick leads with the courage, sensitivity, and missiological passion of Acts 15. His story is a good way to wrap up this chapter.

I will never forget an experience I had attending a worship service at the church he leads. Teenagers served communion while other young adults led the congregation through hymns in both English and Swahili. On one level, it was breathtaking. In that singular moment, I tasted the presence of Jesus spanning cultures, continents, language, and generations. At the same time, on another level, I found myself disturbed by the legacy of Western-led missions. Why were these Kenyan young people leading us in ancient Scottish hymns? Why were the tunes of the songs identical to those I sung as a kid back home? Shouldn't worship in a Kenyan church be something distinctively Kenyan?

Some time later, Patrick was visiting the U.S. and I traveled to Portland, Oregon to meet with him. This time, sitting at a table outside a Barnes and Noble, he shared a frustration over this question. "Why is it that we don't dance in my church? Our culture (in Kenya) dances to celebrate everything. So, why don't we dance in our churches?" I share his concern. Why did we as missionaries transplant the forms of another culture from another era into that environment?

Another time, sitting in his office in Nairobi, Patrick told me about a bold new initiative of his church to adopt a nearby village. He had gone to the national health ministry to find out where the problem of AIDS was worst in Kenya. What he discovered was that the village with the third highest rate of AIDS in the entire country was only a couple hours away. Back at his church Patrick explained his findings and outlined a plan for how congregation could respond.

> *My friends, over the years our colleagues from the West have come to Kenya to help us meet some of the needs that plague our nation. I will always be grateful for their generosity. But, as Kenyans, we have come to believe we don't have the resources necessary to make a difference ourselves. We are so busy with meetings and programs every day here at the church that we are not making a difference in the needs of the world right in front of us. I believe God desires for us to address the brokenness of our land in the name of Christ. It is time to change some of our priorities. God appointed us to be people of redemption and hope. It is time for our church to step up and put the love of Jesus into action for people outside of our church. As for me and my family, we are going to adopt this village and I want you to join us.*

Patrick led his people in something much more than a new ministry project. This represented a massive shift in the life of his church. This moment redefined the way they lived in their community and their nation. It would mean change in the way they managed the church finances, calendar, priorities, and expectations. It was the end of one era and the beginning of a new one.

I wonder what stories would be told if your church and mine found the courage to re-contextualize the way we do life as a church and the way we live in the lost and broken world at our doorstep. In the first century, they did away with circumcision. I wonder what opportunities we would see if we were willing to hold everything we do with an open hand the way they did.

ten

Generation Next

LIKE to think of myself as someone who does not see age differences. I love working with, learning from, and hanging with people of every age. However, when I am in the mood to be honest, I admit that I envision myself as substantially younger than I really am. Not so long ago, I came face to face with the fact that I am just as affected by generational blinders as the next guy.

One of my colleagues—someone whose character and leadership I would follow anywhere without hesitation—is someone I have known and respected since he was in his twenties. Recently, we were talking about leaders and leadership in our mission agency. At one point in the conversation I said something about the emerging crop of younger leaders and included him in that group. But, the truth is, he was thirty-eight years old! How in the world did I miss that? When those of us in leadership positions—including me—speak of someone who is almost forty as a younger leader, we have a real problem. It dawned on me that I am a contributor to the problem as much as I long to be a solution to it. (Darren, thank you for your grace.)

One of the greatest challenges to be answered by every generation is how we develop and empower leaders of the generations that follow us. This challenge is particularly acute right now because of the exodus of younger generations from the church. Parents, pastors, and grandparents alike look at the departure of our young adults with increasing distress. While there are exciting exceptions in many places, the overall trend is that we are losing our kids. The church of the West is hemorrhaging young adults. The faith of our fathers is failing to capture the imagination of our children and grandchildren.

This exodus of younger generations becomes epidemic when you look at the generation gap in church leadership. On the one hand, those in power perceive emerging leaders as lacking experience. On the other hand, younger generations marginalize older leaders they perceive to be out of touch, unable to relate, or simply irrelevant. Regardless of how you slice the situation, the problem is that the gap is growing and we are paying a high price for it.

I am certain you know the axiom: Christianity is never more than one generation away from extinction. We are heading toward a modern day reenactment of the crisis that followed the generation of Joshua and Caleb.

> After that whole generation had been gathered to their fathers, another generation

> grew up who knew neither the Lord nor what
> he had done for Israel.[84]

The Good News of Jesus must be communicated, contextualized, and received anew with every generation. It all starts on a leadership level. The sustainability and capacity for lasting influence of any organization lies in the strength of its leadership bench.

Every generation of established leaders carries the responsibility to develop and empower the generations following behind them. Established leaders hold the keys to a new day. They have the opportunity to raise up, apprentice, and partner with leaders from the very generations we are most worried about. When we raise up those emerging leaders, they will lead the way to reach the generations we are currently losing. Those of us who are getting older do not need to become more hip or more clever in order to reach younger generations. We need to hand the keys to leaders from those generations and let them lead us.

The first century church faced the same challenge. The first generation of leaders was apprenticed directly by Jesus or by those who were. As time went by and the church spread, new leaders were needed. Who would carry the mantle in the generations to come? How were those next generations of leaders to be developed? As that first generation aged and as many of them paid the ultimate price for following Jesus, who would take their place?

The answer for the first century *and for today* is demonstrated by one of the most influential leaders of the

---

New Testament. Most Christians know his name, but I think he deserves more recognition for his contribution than he generally receives. A good argument can be made that his fingerprints are on two-thirds of the New Testament books. His given name was Joe. We know him as Barnabas.

Luke makes a point to detail the pattern of Barnabas' approach with an emerging leader named Saul. In one setting after another, over a span of years, the role of Barnabas in Saul's development paints a picture of what leadership mentoring can look like. Call it mentoring, call it apprenticing, call it anything you like, but the point is the same. One man gave himself to the development of another and the kingdom exploded as a result.

This pattern of leadership development was repeated by Barnabas with John Mark and by Paul with Silas, Timothy, Titus, Epaphroditus, and more. Luke devotes far too much real estate to this relationship for us to see it as anything less than a critical piece of our DNA as a revolutionary people. Leaders in this movement were made not to hoard power or position, but to leverage our positions to multiply other leaders who will extend the reach and impact of the church from one generation to another, from one location to the whole world.

The Genius of Barnabas

Most of us who have been in the evangelical world very long are predisposed to think of Paul's pre-eminent role as the apostle to the Gentiles. Paul is so dominant in our thinking that it is easy to miss the depth and strategy of Barnabas as Paul's mentor. So, follow the trail through Acts with me.

Twenty-one times Luke mentions the names of Barnabas and Paul (or Saul) together as partners. Eleven of those times, Barnabas is mentioned first—as in, "For a whole year *Barnabas* and Saul met with the church [in Antioch]." The first seven of those references name Barnabas first. Of the next fourteen references, though Paul's name is in the first position ten of those times, there remains a back and forth. Paul is recorded first a few times, then Barnabas, then Paul, then Barnabas again. Yes, I know it is a small, technical thing, but this pattern actually makes a profound statement about the nature of their partnership. Barnabas began in the preeminent leadership role but then yielded that position to Paul while remaining alongside and serving together with Paul.[85]

The mentoring partnership established by Barnabas represents the greatest leader development strategy since the days of Jesus. While pastors and ministry leaders I speak with around the world routinely share concern for the need of leaders who will share the ministry load, Barnabas demonstrates a pattern anyone could adopt. The pattern so affected Paul, that his entire ministry going forward mirrors the way God used Barnabas in his own life.

Luke provides us with enough detail that we can do far more than point to Barnabas as a motivating example. By looking closely at the four stages of his relationship with Paul we find a genius to his method. Barnabas offers us an

---

85 When you look at the times Barnabas and Paul are mentioned as a pair, Barnabas is listed first eleven times and Paul is first the remaining ten.

easily reproducible pattern that can be followed by anyone. Consider these four stages with an eye to the opportunities you have for developing the leaders who surround you.

1. SEEK OUT

Everything started when Saul came to Jerusalem after his dramatic conversion on the road to Damascus. We should not be surprised that the believers in Jerusalem saw this as some kind of elaborate hoax. What a great ploy. Infiltrate the church in order to launch more persecution from the inside out. No one trusted Saul and no one could blame them.

"*But Barnabas* took him and brought him to the apostles."[86] While everyone ran for cover, he moved toward Saul. Barnabas had eyes to see God was at work in this man and he wanted to be part of that work.

We see Barnabas demonstrate the same initiative when the apostles sent him to Antioch. Rather than doing ministry alone in Antioch, he saw the potential of bringing Saul to work with him. So, Barnabas left Antioch and traveled 200 miles by foot to search for Saul in his hometown of Tarsus.[87]

Barnabas did not wait for an emerging leader to seek him out for mentoring. He did the seeking. He paid the personal price to travel and search for Saul. Barnabas took the risk that Saul might say, "No, thank you." He did not seek out a non-threatening underperforming leader who would serve as his bag man. He chose someone with tremendous gifts,

---

86 Acts 9.27 (italics added)

87 Acts 11.25. (Tarsus is just inside modern day Turkey, along the coast of the Mediterranean. It is approximately 100 miles each way from Antioch.)

someone who would certainly "pass him up." He sought out Paul at great personal risk in Jerusalem and at great personal inconvenience in Tarsus. It is an approach that tells us we need to give up that passive posture of waiting to be asked to mentor someone. We should take personal initiative to seek out those on whom God has his hand.

Surrounding you are gifted developing leaders. They may be raw, they may have made a few mistakes, but they are made of the right stuff. All it takes is for someone to take the initiative.

2. SPONSOR IN

A sponsor leverages their personal reputation and network to open doors for a developing leader. We saw Barnabas do this with the crowd of people who were afraid of Saul in Jerusalem. At a moment of severe tension Barnabas stepped up as a sponsor and in my words said, "I vouch for this guy. You know me and you know I would never deceive you, so trust me on this one. Trust him because you trust me. I take personal responsibility for Saul." As a result, Saul was able to minister freely for a season in Jerusalem.

We saw Barnabas do it again in Antioch. Luke does not tell us about any of the conversation that happened behind the scenes, but simply that Barnabas traveled to Tarsus to get Saul and brought him back to join in the work in Antioch. Barnabas leveraged his credibility to sponsor Saul into ministry leadership. Whatever Barnabas actually said when he introduced Saul to the congregation, I would suggest that his point was something like this: "I trust God's hand in this man's life and I invite you to trust him with me.

We need his help and I believe God is going to use this man to make a huge difference among us." In short order, Saul stood on his own gifting and reputation. A bit later, when we get to Acts 13, Paul is listed as one of the prophets and teachers in the church of Antioch.

That is the work of a sponsor. They open up their personal network of relationships to the person they are mentoring and leverage their personal reputation to create new opportunities for ministry. Often, emerging leaders have gifts that need to be sharpened through experience, but they lack the track record that will get them in the door to gain that experience.

The down side of age and experience is that those of us who have a little of it recognize how far emerging leaders have to go to move into mature fruitfulness. It is tempting to over-manage them and underestimate the impact they will make in the present. It is nerve-racking to remember the gravity of our own mistakes that could be repeated by those we are mentoring. We forget, that through those opportunities that threw us into the deep end of the pool and those where we failed, some of our most important growth took place.

New opportunities made possible by a sponsor, especially those where the mentor and the apprentice can work in partnership together, offer a way to accelerate leadership development. Consider the response of a gifted thirty-something leader to this conversation about sponsor-mentoring:

> *This opportunity of being sponsored in is the point where I have wished someone walked more closely with me in my own development. Younger leaders often*

convey a sense of confidence, either fake or real, that gives the impression they have some things figured out. Those are the moments in my own development when I found myself most wanting. I have needed older leaders who could help me validate my youth and the areas in which I need to grow at the same time. I need their help offering me experiences to try and then creating space for the feedback loop to process that experience and my learning.[88]

3. SERVE TOGETHER

Classroom-based strategies are manageable, less messy, more controlled, and come with cleaner boundaries, but leaders are not formed in a classroom. Leaders grow in the trenches.

Serving in the trenches together might just be the most easily accessible strategy for anyone who wants to participate in the development of emerging leaders. Established leaders are already working in those trenches where younger leaders need to explore, serve, experiment, and get their hands dirty. If you are serving in leadership in any fashion, you stand at the gateway of tremendous opportunity. Serving together is as simple as inviting someone to join you, sharing responsibility with them, and working alongside one another. Talk, trust, and debrief as you go.

---

88 Travis Collins is a friend and colleague at CRM who directs the work of our Missional Communities Collective. Travis has a special burden for reaching the younger generations being lost. He wrote me this personal note after reading a draft of this chapter.

Jesus developed his disciples like this all the time. For example, on one occasion, he sent seventy-two of his followers ahead of him into all of the villages of Galilee.[89] On another, when the 5,000 needed to be fed, he told his disciples to feed them. When they felt paralyzed by their lack of resources, he performed the miracle in such a way that his disciples were the ones doing the work of the miraculous as they walked among the people.[90]

Luke tells us that after Barnabas returned from Tarsus with Saul, they served together, meeting with the Antioch church for a whole year. A year later, when the Antioch church sent a financial gift to help address the famine in Jerusalem, Barnabas *and* Saul formed the team who delivered the gift and encouragement to the Jerusalem church.

Nothing is more powerful in the development of a leader than the life-on-life exchange that happens while you engage in the work of ministry together. Serving together creates endless opportunities to reflect on critical experiences, sharpen personal values, and nurture a philosophy of ministry. Because adults learn best through repeated cycles of action and reflection, serving in leadership together creates a dynamic learning lab with life-shaping power.

The mentoring impact on emerging leaders explodes when you serve together. If you are the mentor, give them responsibility. Let them lead. Don't control them, but release their creativity. Let them teach you. Let them fail without judgment. If you are the one being mentored, do not assume your mentor knows what you would like to try or what you

---

89 Luke 10.1ff

90 Matthew 14.16-21

feel capable of doing. Suggest ideas, offer to carry more of the load, tell them what you would like to try. Leaders take responsibility for their own mentoring, so stop nursing any expectation that another person can read your mind and take responsibility to initiate conversation together.

4. SEND OFF

When we come to the end of Acts 15, we find two of the most public leaders in the Christian movement embroiled in a disagreement so intense that they chose not to work together any more. On one level, it was a ministry philosophy conflict they couldn't resolve. (Should John Mark be given a second chance or not?) On another level, it represents the maturity of their relationship and marks a graduation of sorts.

As an aside, this is a reminder that the absence of conflict is not always the sign of godliness. We tend to believe that conflict in the church is something we should avoid at all cost. Conflict often serves as refining fire in the development of a leader's character and understanding of ministry. There are ways to focus on issues without turning on each other and when you do, new possibilities emerge.

The final stage of a leadership mentoring relationship means releasing the mentoree. There comes a time when the nature of the relationship needs to graduate into one of peers who no longer work as a team. Too many leaders hold onto their protégés far too long and in so doing, begin to choke their development. The foundation of their relationship is not in question, but *sending off* a mentoree is key to breaking lingering dependency. At the end of the day, Barnabas took

John Mark with him to Cyprus, while Paul took Silas and headed off toward Cilicia.

The sending off stage might also be understood as a return to stage one—*seeking out* new potential mentorees. Barnabas' leader development radar clearly went beyond Saul. Quite some time before this moment of conflict, Barnabas invited John Mark to come with them on their return from Jerusalem to Antioch and then later on their first missionary journey. Barnabas was leaning into that developmental bias of his and wanted to go find John Mark again.

Advance the clock and you find that the results of Barnabas' initiative continue to impact us today. John Mark, the "quitter" for whom Paul had no room, went on to write what most scholars believe was the first of the four Gospels to be recorded. Mathew and Luke later leaned heavily on Mark's initial work as they wrote their gospels for Jewish and Greek audiences respectively. Paul, the former enemy of the church, became the apostle to the Gentiles and was the primary leader of the champion of the Gospel's expansion throughout the Roman Empire. When you add Paul's epistles with the Gospels of Mathew, Mark, and Luke you find the fruit of Barnabas' legacy across two-thirds of the pages in the New Testament.

Mentoring Re-Imagined

I find it interesting that most leaders do not really know how they became one. So, not knowing what else to do, when we want to support the development of other leaders we tend to throw books at them, hoping something sticks. Good books can be powerful tools when introduced at the right time, but they are only part of the process. You will notice that we have said nothing about the content of what Barnabas "taught" Paul. Neither have we said anything about regular meetings nor a slew of other mentoring myths.

Where did we get the notion that mentoring equals a weekly meeting? I have listened to people tell me that they couldn't get involved mentoring someone because they, "don't have time for another weekly commitment." Others get hung up not knowing what curriculum to use. My guess is that our overly structured mindset comes from the dominant academic experiences we share; however, that is not the way mentoring works.

At its core, mentoring is a relational and natural process where one person walks closely with another as they explore developmental issues of common interest. A mentor invites a mentoree to examine all that the mentor has learned and how they learned it. A mentor literally invites another person to walk around in their life to pick the fruit of their experience. A mentoree invites a mentor to poke and prod below the surface of their life looking for underdeveloped traits and skills and knowledge. The process looks nothing like a classroom and a lot like a journey of companions—people who make the sacrifice of accessibility and vulnerability the gift they give one another. Therefore, circumstances of life, shared experiences, and things like hands-on experimentation form the best mentoring curriculum. Concerns like the frequency of meeting and the intensity of attack on the subject at hand are things to be adapted based on need.[91]

---

91 For a more detailed and elaborate look into all the nuances of mentoring, the book *Connecting*, by J. Robert Clinton and Paul Stanley. (NavPress)

It is time for us to confront the narrow ideas and mentoring myths that hold us hostage and re-imagine a more dynamic possibility. It is time to let go of the things that make mentoring a burden and embrace the kind of active partnership we find modeled by Barnabas.

However, before we can fully imagine a different way, most of us need to let go of one or more of the mentoring myths anchored in our subconscious. As myths, these are *not* true. But, they inhibit many of us from offering ourselves as mentors or seeking mentors. When the illusion of these myths causes us to feel inadequate, we disqualify ourselves and leave others underdeveloped. Ask yourself, how many of these myths have you been tripped by?

The Yoda Myth

The belief that a mentor is some über-wise sage who can somehow reveal the secrets of the universe with a few words and a poke in the chest. Not true. Mentors only need to be a few steps further down the road than the mentoree.

The Geezer Myth

The belief that mentors must be significantly older. Not true. You can be mentored by anyone who possesses the experience you need in the area where you need it regardless of age.

The Structure Myth

The belief that mentoring equals a weekly meeting constrained by some content-structured curriculum. A frequent corollary to this myth is the notion that the earlier you meet in the mornings the more godly it is. This way of thinking is so prevalent it deserves extra mention. It is not true. Mentoring is about a relationship. So, whatever rhythms best serve that relationship are the rhythms that matter.

The Guru Myth

The belief that you need one great mentor for life who will speak into every area of your life. Not true. Some of the best mentoring relationships focus on one area in which you need mentoring.

The Mind-Reading Myth

The belief that the right mentor or mentoree will approach you because of what they see in you. Not true. No one reads minds. People do not automatically know what you need or what you are willing to offer. Rather than waiting for someone else to take action, take responsibility for offering and seeking the mentoring you need.

Mentoring is not rocket science. It is a relational exchange where the experience of one person is made available to meet the needs of another. Howard Hendricks is famous for saying it this way: "You can impress people from a distance, but you can only influence people up close."[92] Mentoring means getting up close and letting the Spirit of God use the journey of your life to shape the development of someone else.

One surprising and somewhat disconcerting thing is that although the cumulative impact of a mentoring relationship has incredible power, at any given moment the things you are doing feel ordinary and simple and insignificant. People often give up when they don't experience the fireworks of discovery and assume their efforts are not making a difference.

Personal Gratitude

It would simply be wrong to write a chapter about mentoring and not honor the most significant mentor in my life. Back in the mid-seventies, Stan Leonard became the most important Barnabas in my spiritual formation. Stan was a professor at Biola College.[93] He could have chosen to be satisfied teaching and leading his classes with excellence, but that was not enough. Stan chose to invest in his students.

Stan came to me one day and asked me if I would be willing to join him and a couple other students for lunch every Friday. We brought our brown bags and squeezed into his small office week after week. It's funny, but I don't remember how long we met together or even who all the

---

92 In the tributes to his life, this quote shows up over and over again by those who write of his influence. Howard Hendricks died in February 2013 at the age of 88.

93 Biola College, now Biola University, in La Mirada, California.

people in that lunch group were, but I will never forget the one question Stan always asked, "what has God been teaching you this week?" He did not ask with a stern I'm-here-to police-your-spiritual-life attitude, but from genuine eagerness to share in our learning. His interest was contagious.

I will never forget the way he opened his Bible whenever one of us started talking about a passage of Scripture that had come alive in a new way. With enthusiasm he would lean forward to listen as if he had never thought of the things we were learning. I remember his eyes lighting up as he would exclaim, "Wow!" Then he did this amazing thing. He took out his pen and in the margin of his Bible he wrote the name of the person who made the discovery and the date. He taught me to expect God to show up and speak from his Word every time I open it. And, he taught me to pay attention to when God showed up.

A short time after graduation, Stan invited me to co-teach a class with him at Biola on Inductive Bible Study methods. The school treated me as an adjunct instructor, but I realize it was Stan taking our relationship to another level. He created a way for us to serve together.

I have since moved around the U.S. and into a variety of ministry roles. Stan and his wife, Donna, retired from teaching and moved to Arizona where they served for many years on staff in their home church. Those formative years were quite some time ago, but the imprint they made on my life changed me forever. The role of the Scriptures in my life and in my leadership is the direct result of Stan's investment. All of it was the result of something quite simple. He sought me out. He sponsored me into new opportunities. We served together. And, he blessed me as God sent me onward.

On the corner of my desk at home is a simple gold-colored aluminum baton—the kind used on the track in relay races. It is nothing special and not encased in anything museum-like, but on it are the signatures of my mentor and friend and his wife. It sits there as an active reminder that through the initiative of one man, the Spirit of God handed me a baton. A few years ago I began praying that God would hand a baton through me to at least one hundred other leaders over the next quarter century of my life.

How about you? Who did God send your way as a Barnabas for the sake of your own development? Who are some of the people surrounding you right now who need you as a Barnabas? How are you going to actively participate in closing the leadership and generation gap in order to reach the generations we are losing?

eleven

Spiritual Power

SURROUNDED by shrapnel-scarred buildings and subtle symbols of relentless religious conflict, I walked the streets of Beirut with a Lebanese friend. We were talking about ways God is at work in the Islamic world these days and how that contrasts with what he sees in the West. At one point, mid-stride he turned and said, *"We can't afford to fool around pretending we don't live in a moment of grave urgency. The world is going to hell and so is the church."*[94]

Here in the West we have everything we need to run the enterprise of the church, yet Islam is the fastest growing religion in America. Evangelical Christianity cannot even keep up with the rate of population growth.[95] If the latest

---

94 For security reasons, I need to leave my friend unnamed.

95 Pew Forum on Religion and Public Life, October 9, 2012. This report provides a comprehensive picture, including the fact that between 2007 and 2012, Protestant church affiliation declined 5 percent (p. 13).

technology, great programs, professional staff, and world class buildings were enough to get the job done, the impact of the Western church in the twenty-first century would make the events recorded in Acts seem like tired cable channel reruns. The question is, where do we find true spiritual power that will make the kind of lasting impact we long for the church to make?

The answer?

Prayer.

And yet, declaring that prayer is the key makes me nervous. I get nervous that familiarity with the topic of prayer might lead you to shift over to disinterested autopilot. Nervous that you could react with a ho hum, been there, done that. We all nod to the principle of prayer, but as the focus of groundbreaking advancement, prayer seems to elicit the collective enthusiasm of a big yawn. Even if we can get past our familiarity with prayer, I fear we could corrupt this invitation to dynamic engagement with the God of the universe—the process we call prayer—into another magic pill that is supposed to fix everything. That is, we could turn prayer into nothing more than a transactional formula we think will get us what we want.

In the early church, prayer was an altogether different matter. Prayer was the way bold men and women went to battle in the heavenly realms. It was never the territory of a few, but the constant practice of the many. We find it everywhere in Luke's account.

Throughout our conversation with the leaders of that early church we have looked closely at formative moments that shaped and exposed their DNA—our DNA. However, this final strand of DNA is not to be found in a singular moment—it is found everywhere on every page of their life together. It is found in the personal lives of leaders and in congregational gatherings. It is connected to supernatural intervention and to mundane decision making. It may sound like familiar territory for most of us, and yet, the way they prayed stands in stark contrast to the typical prayer meeting most of us are accustomed to.

We need to be honest. No established Christian would argue against the value of prayer, but in practice we often relegate it to the role of a ceremonial or side line activity. So many other things are urgent and important. Bold public initiatives, new ministry activities, and special events get the greatest amount of energy and attention. We rarely look to prayer as the most important or most strategic work of kingdom advancement. It is acknowledged as powerful, but treated as a religiously tame ritual. We could not be more wrong.

Prayer might be the least tame thing we ever do!

This final piece of our DNA could be the most important of them all. We were born to live with a spiritual power that confounds the wise. All the strands of our DNA shape our revolutionary potential, but the spiritual power of our impact is unleashed through prayer. When God entrusted us with his mission in the world, he wired us for dependency on him. In that posture of dependency we discover true spiritual authority.

The power and impact of our ministry will never be found in the quality of our preaching, programs, or personnel, but in the depth and consistency of our prayer. There is no manmade pathway to revolutionary power and influence. Prayer is it. There is no plan B.

The thing is, it was not just *that* the early church prayed, but the way they prayed calls for us to stand up and take notice. Their prayers were bold and direct and supernatural in scope. They had the audacity to ask God to do things that would be clearly recognized, or not. They *way* they prayed, *when* they prayed, and *what they saw* God do paints a different picture than what most of us experience. The revolutionary impact of the Church was empowered by the pattern of their prayer. It is a pattern that will lead us into a new normal.

Bold

I have no idea what words you would use to describe the language and patterns of your own prayer life, but I know that the congregational and small group prayers I have heard over the past few decades are rarely anything close to bold. It seems we are conditioned to pray with soft language and abstract phrases. We use words of tentative request and temper them even further with "just" and "may." While working on this chapter, I heard a worship leader this past week pray these words, "Lord, may we mean every word that we sing." What was he actually saying? I don't mean to criticize and don't mean to nitpick, but I think his prayer is an example of the milieu of our common prayer life.

Prayer is more than the words we use, but at the same time, the words we choose are an indicator of posture behind them. The prayers of this first century church sounded quite different from the ones we pray. Rather than a timid group of people acting as if they are afraid to interrupt a busy and powerful ruler, they engaged in prayer like Roman gladiators taking new territory.

Recall the imagery from movies like *Gladiator*? Roman legions advanced upon their enemies by linking arms and overlapping their large shields to form a seamless line. When the enemy attacked with bows and arrows, the second line of soldiers would create an impenetrable cover of shields above the heads of the line in front of them. As a result, a long wall of solid steel advanced step after step to take the ground in front of them. This early church prayed in a way that sounds more like gladiators taking on enemy territory than a polite religious tea party. Listen for yourself.

In Acts 4, the Jewish authorities "seized" Peter and John and in a classic attempt at intimidation, threw them in jail overnight. The next day, those leaders dragged Peter and John into their council chambers and ordered them to stop speaking or teaching in Jesus' name. In response to this escalating pressure, the prayer meeting that followed is quite amazing. These believers did *not* pray for protection or safety. They did not cry out complaining about how unfair and unjust this was. They did not pray anything remotely tentative. Instead they prayed about taking new ground.

> Now Lord, consider their threats and enable your servants to speak your word with great boldness. Stretch out your hand to heal and perform miraculous signs and wonders through the name of your holy servant Jesus.[96]

---

96 Acts 4.29-30

They prayed for the boldness and power to defy the direct order that already got them arrested and flogged! The answer to their prayer? An earthquake! Or, more precisely, a single-building quake. They prayed for boldness and God applauded. The building shook, they were filled with the Holy Spirit, and they left that place speaking the word of God boldly.[97] The whole scenario makes me smile. I wonder how our prayer lives might change if the building shook when we prayed.

They expected things to happen because of their prayer. Although Ephesians 3.20-21 was not yet written, they showed us what it looks like to expect God to work in ways beyond anything we can ask or imagine. And, they did it without becoming arrogant. Their prayer life demonstrated desperate dependency on the hand of the King without crossing the line and treating God like a vending machine.

Constant

No surprise therefore, that with conviction like this, they prayed all the time. As a matter of fact, the very first description Luke provided about life in this early church told us that they "joined together constantly in prayer."[98]

They prayed before making decisions, they prayed for people in need, they prayed in response to crises, they prayed when they needed supernatural intervention, they prayed over the appointment of leaders, they prayed in

---

97 Acts 4.31

98 Acts 1.14

organized prayer gatherings, and they prayed as a normal part of daily life. Prayer was more than a special event and more than the appropriate way to start Christian gatherings. By my count there are at least twenty-nine specific instances where their prayer life is referenced in the book of Acts. The practice of prayer weaves throughout every facet of life for this community, revealing the real source of their spiritual power.

Think for a moment about how this is different from much of our contemporary experience—including my own default as a ministry leader. When leadership teams gather to address the business, direction, and plans for the ministry, how much of that time do they spend praying? When our people are gathered, we carry out highly sophisticated programs, services, and special events, but how much time do we devote to prayer?

If prayer is the least tame thing we might ever do, doesn't it make sense that it should become one of the things we do most?

A godly and wise friend of mine who runs a successful business challenged me with a profound observation one day over coffee. "As leaders, we are always thinking about strategic opportunities and tasks that need to be accomplished. But, what if time we spend engaged in prayer and communion with Jesus is actually the time of greatest productivity—the time when we accomplish the most?"

Supernatural

I don't know what you imagine happens when you pray, but one thing I do know is that we are not just speaking words into the air. Prayer is a conversation with the King of the universe—a King who has turned his ears to hear everything we have to say.[99] We are not just saying words of a ritual that does something therapeutic for our souls. In prayer we step into heavenly realms to engage the fullness of reality.

Reality encompasses both the natural *and* the supernatural realms. Think about it: what we see with our eyes is only a small slice of the true scope of all that is going on. If we could see reality through God's eyes, we would discover that what we see in the natural realm is only a small fraction of reality. If we could see reality from God's perspective, we would instantly and forever understand that we "do not struggle against flesh and blood, but against the rulers…authorities…powers of this dark world and against the spiritual forces of evil in the heavenly realms."[100]

If we saw reality as it really is, we would surrender any notion that we could accomplish the transformational work of Jesus through the power of our programming. Programs and other intentional efforts that shape ministry are great things. But on a deeper, truer level, the redemption and transformation of people's lives, families, neighborhoods, and even of cities and nations is a supernatural process. Think about the deeper longings that simmer within us for the impact of the church. We want Jesus to be seen. We want

---

99 Psalms 116.1-2

100 Ephesians 6.12

multitudes of new people to follow him. We want his justice to reign, and more. All of those longings face supernatural opposition that can only be addressed through supernatural means.

When the early church prayed, things happened that cannot be explained naturally. The first thing that we notice was the number of miraculous healings. Peter and John on their way to prayer in the temple, healed a man who had been crippled from birth.[101] After the believers prayed in Acts 4 for boldness and for the ability to heal and perform miraculous signs and wonders, we read that "the apostles performed many miraculous signs and wonders among the people," a direct fulfillment of their prayer. "As a result, people brought the sick into the streets…so that at least Peter's shadow might fall on some of them as they passed by. Crowds gathered… bringing their sick and those tormented by evil spirits, and all of them were healed."[102] Later, Paul prays over Tabitha and sees her raised from the dead![103]

While the connection between prayer and the miraculous in that first century might be familiar, have you noticed the frequency in which God shows up through divine visitation while people are praying? Eight different times in the book of Acts, Luke shows us that *while they were praying* God came and met with them. For example, while Cornelius was in his house praying about three in the afternoon one day, "a man in shining clothes stood before me." That angel

101 Acts 3.1ff

102 Acts 5.12 and 14-16

103 Acts 9.40

told Cornelius to send for Peter.[104] Two or three days' journey away, Peter was up on the roof praying when God spoke to him through that dramatic vision of food, showing him that no man was to be considered unclean.[105] Not long after his conversion, Paul was in the temple praying when he "fell into a trance and saw the Lord speaking," warning him to leave Jerusalem immediately because of a plot against his life.[106] We have already talked about what took place during that time of worship in Antioch—the Holy Spirit spoke to the church. At one point when Paul and Silas were in prison, while they were "worshipping and praying," an earthquake happened and their chains miraculously feel off.[107]

Over and over again, Luke points us to the pattern of supernatural intervention that is directly connected to prayer. The connections are too dramatic and too numerous to be coincidental. The closer we look, the more we see that the natural work of prayer is the work of supernatural engagement.

I am curious about why we see so little of the supernatural in the Western church of the twenty-first century. I do not have any research, only questions. But I wonder about it. I wonder if we have been so blinded by a naturalistic worldview that we fail to notice how badly we need supernatural intervention. I wonder if our advanced training and amazing technologies have lulled us into

---

104 Acts 10.3-8, 30-33

105 Acts 10.9-20

106 Acts 22.17-18

107 Acts 16.25

thinking that we can carry it from here. I even wonder if it is as simple as "we don't have because we do not ask."[108]

Biased for Action

And, just in case we are tempted to misunderstand all this talk of boldness and the supernatural to see prayer as something "otherworldly," we need to stop and acknowledge it is nothing of the sort. When we look at the prayer life of this early church we find that prayer and action were inseparable.

How many times have you been in a meeting grappling with a difficult decision when someone in the group brought the tension to a halt by saying, "we should pray about it." Now, who could criticize a suggestion for prayer at a time like this? It sounds on the surface exactly like the very point of this chapter. However, I cannot count the number of times I've heard a call to prayer used as a way to avoid the tension or risk of making a decision. After all, as long as we are praying about it, we do not have to take action.

This was not their way. Prayer and action were inseparable twins. Here are two easy examples. First, after identifying two possible candidates to replace Judas, they prayed and immediately drew lots. Luke writes of both in the same breath because, I believe, their drawing of lots was as much a step of dependence on the Spirit to guide them as was their prayer. The two steps were seamless. Second, when the Holy Spirit told the church in Antioch to deploy Barnabas and Saul, the church prayed and sent them off.

---

108 James 4.2

They prayed, and boom, they acted, giving away two of the most important leaders in their church to a mission fraught with danger and the unknown.

Somehow, in our contemporary experience, we divorce the two. We embrace action as something tangible and practical, the place for active involvement. The domain of human responsibility. Meanwhile, we treat prayer as an intangible activity for the religious domain. Prayer is polite and well-intentioned, but not the domain of real work. Prayer is a spiritual thing and perceived as impractical, even irrelevant to the regular tasks and decisions of life and business.

Take a hard look at how often we separate what we see God responsible for and what we see ourselves responsible for. It is easy to see why prayer gets relegated to spiritual spaces or personal crises. We put our contemporary spin on the old Gnostic heresy, dividing our view of life into the secular and the sacred. We see things of the Spirit as disconnected from things of the flesh. We marginalize what we see as God's concerns to those things *we* consider spiritual. It is as if we come to God periodically to talk to him about "God stuff" and then walk away saying, "Thanks, I'll take it from here."

The sense of expectancy that drove their constant life of prayer creates a backdrop to one of the truly humorous moments in the Scriptures. Just after we hear that the King Herod arrested and killed James, the brother of John, Peter is arrested. The tide was changing and the believers in Jerusalem had every right to fear that Peter would be next. So, they gathered that evening at the home of Mary, the mother of James and John, for a night of concerted prayer. In the middle of the night, while they were praying (sound familiar?), an angel visits Peter in prison and secrets him out away from danger. So, Peter goes immediately to Mary's house, eager to get off the street, unsure how soon the guards would take notice and begin a manhunt. He knocks on the door and the servant opens the peephole to see who is making such a fuss. Then seeing Peter, she whips around and runs back into the house to tell the group of God's dramatic answer to their prayer—leaving Peter exposed and vulnerable as a fugitive in the street. I guess even the most expectant prayer warriors can be surprised by the speed and boldness by which God acts.

More than a Transaction

At the front end of this chapter, I expressed my fear that another chapter on prayer could be met with a big yawn of familiarity. Now, at the back end of the chapter, I have an entirely different fear. I worry that by talking about the potential of prayer and the ways they prayed, it could seem that I advocate a transactional view of prayer. Nothing could be further from the truth.

God is not a vending machine whose levers are pulled by some magic prayer formula. He is majesty and mystery. He moves according to his will. Furthermore, he invites us into a life of intimacy that is so much bigger than anything we could ever conceive of, let alone formulate into focused prayer. Prayer is the language of relationship, not a mechanism for getting what we want. We have much to learn about praying like they did, but that does not mean prayer is   an equation that produces results at our demand. Prayer can be active as much as it can be quiet listening prayer.[109]

Thus we come to one of the great paradoxes of prayer. Prayer is the language of relationship with our God who already knows everything we long to bring to him. At the same time, prayer is the practice of engagement and partnership with him in the battles fought in the realm of the supernatural. He doesn't need us, yet he chooses to work in concert with our prayer.

We could devote endless energy trying to dissect the nuances of prayer: however, the point is that the early church lived a life of prayer and their prayer life is inseparable from their spiritual power. Without ever shifting into a transactional posture, they prayed in ways that call us to a life of prayer that is revolutionary. Constant. Bold. Supernaturally focused. Action oriented. They prayed and the world was changed. It is not an equation that produces the right results if we plug the right pieces in. Things happen when God's people pray that do not happen when they don't.

In this modern era there are many things that local churches are known for. There are many things we emphasize. But, we cannot look at the prayer life of those early believers and walk away thinking we can achieve revolutionary influence on the world with humanly engineered strategies.

Stories are beginning to leak out about profound movements of evangelism and church planting among some

---

109 There is such a wealth of good writing on the disciplines of prayer that it feels wholly inadequate to skim that subject here. However, to address more here would take us far beyond the scope of this chapter. If you need a place to begin that conversation, let me suggest you consider the writings of Ruth Haley Barton.

of the hardest to reach segments of the Hindu and Muslim populations in India. These movements of God are happening in parts of the country most hostile to Christianity—territories where Christians are harassed and killed. These are the parts of the country once considered the graveyard of missionaries.

People are coming to Christ by the thousands and thousands through grassroots movements. Church planters with simple, basic training travel by bicycle from village to village. Many work full-time jobs in addition to their church planting efforts. They have none of the resources we deem essential for a church here in the Western world. They lack well-trained clergy with post-graduate degrees. They don't have nice church buildings in which to gather people. Programming resources are essentially non-existent. And, people are coming to Christ in amazing numbers.

So, what makes the difference?

One of those church planters reports, they pray three hours a day. Every day. They pray by name for every one of the people they are trying to reach. They pray for every one of the leaders in these churches being started. They pray for every one of their disciples. They do not know how it would even be possible to do this work without a minimum of three hours in prayer every day.

Does it sound like a different world from the normal experience of Church in the West?

The point is, we are not called to live as a better version of a healthy social club. We live as the Body of Christ entrusted with the mission of Christ deployed into a world that needs to know him. We cannot accomplish in the flesh what is fundamentally a work of the Spirit. And, we cannot accomplish the lasting work of the Spirit in any other way than through prayer.

Prayer as a Prophetic Posture

Paul wrote that God uses the foolish things to confound the wise.[110] What could be more foolish in the twenty-first century than to make a claim that prayer may be the strategic path to change the world? We live in a day that loves big and bold and impressive initiatives. We look to big budget Hollywood to grab our attention. We love the big personality leader. We think of important global initiatives as those who will be championed by people with money and power. We expect anything worthwhile to come packaged in four-color glossy branding. Prayer simply does not fit that bill. Prayer feels archaic.

And therein lies the prophetic power of a counter culture people. Just as prayer might be the least tame thing we ever do, prayer is the last thing a revolutionary movement in the twenty-first century would depend on. Unless that movement bears the name of Christ. When the people of Christ start living lives of radical commitment to prayer, we display an entirely different way.

What if local churches started seeing the explosive work of God for no other reason than they prayed? What if people in our churches started praying in extravagant ways that looked crazy-stupid to our culture? What if you showed up at work and when people asked you to explain

---

110 1 Corinthians 1.27-28

the revolutionary things taking place, you told them it was only because of the way your church prays?

In 1976, J. Edwin Orr, a renowned student of revivals in history, gave one of the most powerful talks ever given on "the role of prayer in spiritual awakening."[111] In his dramatically understated way, Dr. Orr stood at the podium and simply talked about the miraculous work God has done in history as a result of concerted, united, sustained prayer. The opening words of his presentation were a quote from Dr. A.T. Pierson.

> There has never been a spiritual awakening in any country or locality that did not begin in united prayer.

There is no evidence anywhere that God's methods have changed. At our core, we are a people whose DNA wires us to live in desperate dependence through prayer. The consistent work of prayer and the posture behind it releases spiritual power—the power that unleashes the revolutionary impact we long for.

---

111 "The Role of Prayer in Spiritual Awakening," by Dr. J. Edwin Orr. Originally presented at the National Congress on Prayer in Dallas, TX. 1976. © Campus Crusade for Christ, 1977.

twelve

Reclaiming Our Birthright

A **LONG** time ago, in an age when I think dinosaurs still roamed the earth, my son was in kindergarten. I remember him coming home every day with adorable stories of how the world looked through the eyes of a five year old. One of the stories I will never forget was his report about the day he was asked what his father did for a living. When that question came to Ryan, he stood up and announced with all the certainty of a budding theologian, "He talks and somebody sings."

That's it? The calling of my life and the revolutionary nature of the church reduced to "He talks and somebody sings"?

Of course that's not what it means to be a pastor. Ryan was five. We found his comments funny at the time and still laugh at them today. All the same, in a painful way, his description is not far from typical perceptions about the church. When people think about the church, they generally think about the worship service and when they think about the worship service, in most cases, music and a sermon are forefront.

I have argued throughout this book for the very nature of our birthright as a church and as followers of Christ. We were born again into life as a revolutionary force intended to transform the world. I do not mean revolutionary as in a frenzied crowd of angry students at a political rally, but a countercultural, life-giving community that brings a redemptive presence into a desperate world.

I did not choose "revolutionary" for dramatic effect, but because it represents the life we were intended to live and the impact we were intended to make. Days of explosive growth are not limited to ancient history. Pentecost-like days and seasons are possible in any generation and any culture. Our potential for revolutionary impact goes beyond the numbers of people who will become followers of Christ to include the radical transformation of communities and cultures as the Gospel invades a broken world. I believe God intends for cities to be filled with great joy as a result of the way we live in the world.[112] I believe we have been given as a gift to a needy world and by living out that assignment the world will be caught by surprise.

The problem is *we have been conned.*

---

112 Acts 8.8 speaks of the great joy that filled a town in Samaria after Philip ministered there.

Somewhere along the line, we exchanged our birthright for a counterfeit. We were sold a bill of goods through distortions, such as …

- Maturity in Christ is measured by mastery of Bible knowledge and doctrine.
- Being a disciple means something above and beyond being a normal Christian.
- It is possible to follow Jesus fully without living as a witness among the lost.
- Engaging the poor or marginalized outside of the church is not for everyone.
- The church is primarily about nurture and care for members.
- Pastoral ministry is about nurturing the flock and trusting others to minister to those beyond our walls.

A loving God who desperately loves us *and* loves the world invites us to join him in doing what matters most in that world and, in the process, to discover what matters most in life. Living for the sake of other people just makes sense. The allure of self-serving environments focused on caring for me never live up to their seductive promise.

The biblical picture is that Christians are followers of Christ, followers of Christ are disciples, and disciples are missionaries. Choose whatever term you like, they all refer to the one and only life Jesus intended. Extend the implications of that reality and you find that to be his church is to be a community of missionaries deployed into the world for the sake of the world. Anything other than that is a counterfeit.

> If your church is full of members, you get an occasional missionary. If your church is full of missionaries, the rest is just about geography.[113]

Our Birthright

During the days when I was writing this final chapter, I had dinner and a fascinating conversation with a good friend who is in his late twenties. Among the smorgasbord of topics we picked our way through that evening, we talked about a novel we had both recently read. This was one of those novels that wove questions of global crisis and social responsibility into the story line. So, we talked about it. Then my friend asked, "Do you ever wonder what it would take to make you radically change the way you live your life?"

He went on. "I know a tragic accident that threatens your life or leaves you permanently disabled would make anyone rethink their life, but what about something that was not crisis driven? What could be so urgent or compelling on the positive side, that it would cause you to realign the priorities and patterns of your life?"

His question got me thinking and surfaced what I find to be the most moving reality of our birthright. I put my response this way. Imagine that the God of the universe— the eternal creator and ruler over all that is—sat down in a

---

113 Erwin R, McManus, *Seizing Your Divine Moment.* Thomas Nelson, Nashville, 2002. p.166.

chair next to you and spoke to you in a very personal way. "I have a plan to change the world and I want to ask you to join me as a partner in that effort. I want you to help me make it happen."

That invitation is precisely what God says to each one of us. It may not be the way we normally talk about the Christian life, but it is the invitation of God throughout the Scriptures. Our birthright as Children of God goes beyond a relationship with the Father to include partnership with him in the redemptive plan for which Jesus gave his life.

God's plan positioned his people as key players in his global agenda from the beginning of time. Out of the gate, he gave Adam the assignment to name all the animals. He gave Adam and Eve the job of tending the garden. He called the people of Israel to be a light to the nations. He declared, "If you repent, I will restore you so that you may serve me."[114] In the New Testament, Jesus called his disciples to join him in order to become fishers of men. Through Paul, he identifies us as ambassadors of reconciliation. Over and over and over again, the same theme emerges. As the children of God, we are more than recipients of his grace—we are ambassadors of reconciliation. Biblically, there is no such thing as a Christian life defined by membership in an organization.

Our birthright as Children of God is defined not only by restored intimacy with our creator, but is equally an invitation into partnership with him in the work that matters more than anything else on the planet: the redemption of a lost and broken world. To be a follower of Christ is to be a participant at his side in everything he is up to in the world. It

---

114 Jeremiah 15.19

Perspective: Thinking Locally-Globally

I recognize that I write from and for those with a predominantly American experience. At the same time, this conversation about the life of the church is not about our life in America; it is about the way we live as partners in the local-global movement of God.

When we look at the world from a global perspective, it becomes clear that every local church lives as a partner in a worldwide enterprise. No single local community of believers is responsible for the whole planet, but God assigned each one to one primary place. Living locally with a global perspective shapes multiple facets of the way think.

First, our assignment as the church does not look one way at home and another way when we talk about missionaries assigned somewhere else in the world. All of us share the responsibility of being and bringing Good News to a lost world. Missions is a way of life no matter where we are on the planet. We can no longer talk about the role of the local church as one of training and care for believers in a way that is distinct from the role of missionaries whose role is to move into unreached territory. There is overwhelming "unreached" territory all around us. The mission of the church does not change when we cross the big blue water.

A second thought, we participate in the global work of Christ best when we accept our responsibility for the local work before us. When the people of a local church are engaged in the missionary work of reaching their immediate community, they begin to better understand the challenges and strategies of cross-cultural missionaries. When a local church prioritizes its own Jerusalem and Judea they are is an offer so amazing and so life-altering that to understand it is to be left breathless.

Yeah, But ...

If following Jesus means following him on mission as much as it means following him into deep fellowship with the Father, then all of our priorities as a church are affected. If his mission lives at the center of his heart, it lives at the center of our identity and our assignment. We cannot afford to look at our priorities through any other lens. We are a community of missionaries assigned to the mission field we call home.

However, having said this, I have to expect this argument creates a significant "yeah, but ..." tension. Yeah, we are called to be witnesses, but we are also called to love one another. Yeah, we might be a missionary people, but we are also told to equip and edify one another. Yeah, we want to prioritize engagement in the world around us, but the New Testament also brims with "one another" instructions.[115]

This tension between mission and "member care" cannot be minimized. Both dynamics occupy the same space at the same time. However, we need not adopt an either/or posture. I am not suggesting that we don't care for our people. But I am suggesting that pastoral care serves a greater priority: mobilization for engagement in the world. The reality of being human and being a community of broken people means we

---

115 For starters, you can find some of the "one another" exhortations in Romans 12.10, 12.16, 15.7; Ephesians 4.2, 4.32; Colossians 3.13; 1 Thessalonians 5.11; and Hebrews 10.24-25.

will never finish caring for personal needs. If we place caring for our people as the first job to be accomplished, we will never get to the task of giving ourselves away for the sake of others. If we place deployment on mission as the step after people have been fully trained, we will never deploy people out into the world. There will always be urgent needs in the congregation. There will always be more training and learning that would be helpful. None of us will every fully "arrive."

Think of it this way. An army has hospitals, training schools, counseling centers, recreational leagues, marching bands, and even golf courses, but an army is not fundamentally a hospital, a university, a recreational center or any of these specialty services. An army is a military unit built for a mission and *everything* they do is designed to advance that mission.

For years, the default posture of the church has been to understand our assignment as chaplains of a Christian heritage in a land we perceived as predominantly Christian. In contrast, the consistent message of our brothers and sisters in the book of Acts is that we are not chaplains preserving anything. Chaplains care for what is. A missionary movement exists to extend the Good News of Jesus to as many people in as many communities as humanly possible. And, the unexpected paradigm shift that occurs when we live this way is that through our engagement in the mission of Jesus, our lives are transformed as much or more as when we are studying about Jesus.

better able to enter into partnership with those who take up the mantle to reach Samaria and the uttermost parts of the earth. This local-global way of living obliterates a black and white marginalizing view of the world—home versus "the field." It births a recognized continuity from our door to the farthest corners of the world. The ways we pray and support those called to cross cultures are transformed when we experience the hardships and sacrifices of reaching into the lost and unjust world at our doorstep.

Thirdly, owning our part in the local-global mission of Christ calls for a courageous willingness to give away our best and brightest leaders. Just as the church of Antioch sent off their "senior pastor" and brightest rising star of new leadership, it is time for the church of the twenty-first century to sacrifice the very people we would like to "keep for ourselves." By living as a local community of missionaries, we actively shape our children and our emerging leaders with a native bias for missional engagement. We apprentice people to participate in the global agenda of Jesus by the way we do life locally. Giving away our best and brightest will require a whole new level of sacrifice within local churches.

Finally, realigning the perspective and practice of local congregations calls for courageous and risk-taking leadership. The implications unleashed by this way of thinking represent a massive shift in language, priorities, and daily behavior for the average local church. Throughout our conversation with the leaders of that first century, we have talked about this shift from members to missionaries, but at the end of the day, making this shift comes down to leadership. It requires living before the Audience of One rather than the expectations and applause of the crowd.[116] And, it can only be accomplished if change in the lifestyle of leaders precedes any attempt to change the priorities of a congregation.

The church does not live by one set of priorities here at home and another when established in a foreign culture. We follow the same Savior who is on the same mission with the same priorities regardless of geography or culture.

Bottom of the Ninth

It is time to fight for the church. Not to fight for preserving the way things used to be and not to fight for mere organizational survival. It is time to fight for the church that needs to be in order to reach the world as it really is.

I grew up playing baseball and if you played much ball as a kid, I think you know the dream. In my version, the Dodgers were in the World Series and asked me to suit up to help the team. It was Game 7, bottom of the ninth, two outs, men on base and we were down by one. The manager calls me over, hands me a bat, and sends me to the plate. "Son, this is your day." What a great moment! (Never mind that I was in junior high or high school, depending on the iteration of the dream. This was *my* dream.) As a baseball player, when the game is on the line, you want to be at the plate with the bat. You want the chance to affect the outcome of the game. It is the opportunity of a lifetime.

I am not suggesting it is bottom of the ninth in an eschatological sense, but I do believe that when it comes to

---

116 This concept and the very best description of it come from Os Guiness' book *The Call.* Thomas Nelson, 2003.

the church in our generation, the game is on the line and we have the chance to change the outcome. We live in a decisive moment in history and in the church. It is a time when everything seems to be in flux, yet a moment that is pregnant with opportunity. The opportunity before us is ripe with hope.

The prophetic words of Mordecai could be aptly spoken over us.

> "Who knows but that you have come to the royal position for such a time as this."[117]

In the same way, the pattern of God's redemptive strategy Paul declared to the Athenians applies to us today.

> [God] determined the times set for them and the exact places where they should live. God did this so that men would seek him and perhaps reach out for him and find him, though he is not far from each one of us.[118]

Rather than despair over the loss of all that is changing, it is time to embrace the redemptive possibilities that surround us and courageously become the church we were always meant to be. With a world in flux, we have an unprecedented opportunity to step up as God's primary delivery system of hope and healing in a broken world.

---

117 Esther 4.14

118 Acts 17.26-27

It Starts with You ... *and Me*

While this is a book about the church, it is simultaneously a book about the way you and I live our lives. It has not been a conversation about theory, but a call to action.

A friend of mine did me the favor of reading a majority of this book in its first draft form. What moved me most in our debrief together was the comment he made after we had finished formally talking about the book. As we put our notes aside, he looked me in the eye and said, "This is much more than a book about how the church should live. Every chapter spoke to me about the way *I* need to live."

Don't worry about pointing fingers at others. Get started by taking a look at your own life. What have you settled for? What have you heard the Spirit of God stirring in you? Are there any patterns or beliefs for which you need to repent, any areas that call for a realignment of your priorities, or any new steps of obedience that demand tremendous courage and risk? If we are going to unleash a revolutionary way forward for the church, it begins with us.

There are scores of people, communities,
and entire nations
waiting on the other side of our obedience.

About the Author

GARY Mayes, D.Min, is Executive Director of ChurchNext for Church Resource Ministries (CRM). In this role, he leads the work of more than 75 staff on twelve teams who work with ministry leaders to transform the posture and impact of the church. Before joining CRM in '97, Gary served in local pastoral ministry for twenty years. He has developed resources used by CRM staff and other leaders around the world, and is called upon to train, coach, and consult with pastors, ministry leaders, and their churches across the evangelical spectrum. He was privileged to play an integral part in the launch of CRM's indigenous and independent partner in Africa, Harvest Leaders' Network.

This is Gary's fourth book and will soon be joined by a 20th anniversary updated edition of his book, *Now What? Resting in the Lord when Life Doesn't Make Sense.*

He and his wife Margaret have been married more than 35 years and live in Santa Ana, CA.

Gary writes a blog on lessons about the intersection of life and leadership: www.aboutleading.com.

To contact Gary: www.garymayes.me.

CRM EMPOWERING LEADERS

CHURCH Resource Ministries is a global movement that empowers leaders to revitalize the impact of the Church, take new ground beyond the reach of the existing church, and bring transformation among the poor—so that, disciples are made and communities are transformed.

More than 400 CRM missionaries live and minister in urban, suburban, and rural settings around the world. We believe that a different future is possible and that the Church is key to God's strategy for that redemptive potential. Our mission is inspired by a passion for the Church *that is* as well as a vision for the Church *that can be*. Our work is carried out by staff who seek to minister out of the primary values of character, relationship, competency, and spiritual passion. The heart of our strategy is developing leaders committed to both.

Since beginning in 1980, CRM has expanded to more than 30 nations and launched partner organizations led by national leaders in ten countries.

For more about CRM: www.crmleaders.org.

22478854R00120

Made in the USA
Charleston, SC
24 September 2013